DPT

ALLEN COUNTY PUBLIC LIBRARY

**FRIENDS
OF ACPL**

3 1833 04736 9951

D1318553

Animal Rights

Animal Rights

Look for these and other books in the Lucent Overview series:

Abortion

Acid Rain

Adoption

AIDS

Bigotry

The Brain

Cancer

Chemical Dependency

Censorship

Cities

Civil Liberties

Cloning

Cults

The Death Penalty

Democracy

Divorce

DNA on Trial

Drug Abuse

Drugs and Sports

Drug Trafficking

Eating Disorders

Endangered Species

Epidemics

Environmental Groups

Espionage

Ethnic Violence

Euthanasia

Family Violence

Gambling

Gangs

Gay Rights

Global Resources

Gun Control

Hazardous Waste

Health Care

Homeless Children

Human Rights

Illegal Immigration

The Internet

Juvenile Crime

Mental Illness

Militias

Money

Multicultural America

Obesity

Oil Spills

The Palestinian-Israeli Accord

Paranormal Phenomena

Police Brutality

Population

Poverty

The Rebuilding of Bosnia

Saving the American Wilderness

Schools

Sexual Harassment

Sports in America

Suicide

Terrorism

The U.S. Congress

The U.S. Presidency

Violence in the Media

Violence Against Women

Women's Rights

Zoos

Animal Rights

by Leanne K. Currie-McGhee

LUCENT BOOKS

An imprint of Thomson Gale, a part of The Thomson Corporation

Detroit • New York • San Francisco • San Diego • New Haven, Conn. • Waterville, Maine • London • Munich

On cover: A monkey is confined in a bottle during a research experiment.

© 2005 Thomson Gale, a part of The Thomson Corporation.

Thomson and Star Logo are trademarks and Gale and Lucent Books are registered trademarks used herein under license.

For more information, contact
Lucent Books
27500 Drake Rd.
Farmington Hills, MI 48331-3535
Or you can visit our Internet site at http://www.gale.com

ALL RIGHTS RESERVED.
No part of this work covered by the copyright hereon may be reproduced or used in any form or by any means—graphic, electronic, or mechanical, including photocopying, recording, taping, Web distribution, or information storage retrieval systems—without the written permission of the publisher.

Every effort has been made to trace the owners of copyrighted material.

LIBRARY OF CONGRESS CATALOGING-IN-PUBLICATION DATA

Currie-McGhee, L.K. (Leanne K.)
    Animal rights / by Leanne K. Currie-McGhee.
        p. cm. — (Overview)
    Includes bibliographical references and index.
    ISBN 1-56006-548-6 (hardcover : alk. paper)
    1. Animal rights—Juvenile literature. I. Title. II. Series: Lucent overview series.
    HV4708.C86 2004
    179'.3—dc22
                                                    2004010562

Printed in the United States of America

Contents

Introduction

IN 1987 JENNIFER Graham's high school classmates dubbed her the "frog girl." People throughout the United States soon knew Graham, a fifteen-year-old tenth grader at Victor Valley High School in California, by the same name. Graham made headlines across the country because she refused to dissect a frog for a school assignment. "I'm not squeamish or emotional . . . I don't want to have any part in it,"[1] Graham explained. She said she objected to the killing of animals for research.

Frog dissection was a required science assignment at Graham's high school. Graham refused to complete the assignment because she believed that by doing so she would be condoning the senseless killing of animals. After Graham refused to dissect the frog, her principal told her that she could skip the assignment, but it would be deducted from her grade. This was not acceptable to Graham because she needed a high grade to go to college.

Graham sued the school district for not allowing her to complete an alternative assignment. When the public heard about her case, many people wrote letters to her showing their support. Her court case was settled without trial and her original grade in class, an "A," was reinstated.

Right to life

For years, middle and high school students like Graham have been required to dissect frogs, cats, fetal pigs, rats, and snakes in biology classes. Approximately 6 million animals are dissected each year in schools. Many school officials and teachers support dissection because they believe it gives students a firsthand study of biology and anatomy, fosters an interest in science, and may lead students to careers in medicine or research. However, like Graham, several students have protested against dissection, believing it violates an animal's rights.

Graham believes in the animal rights philosophy that animals are born with inherent rights, such as the right to live their lives without being abused by humans. The goal of the animal rights movement is to stop all uses of animals that cause them pain or death. Writes Tom Regan, coauthor of *The Animal Rights Debate*, "The [animal rights] movement's goals include the total abolition of commercial animal agriculture, the total abolition of the fur industry, and the total abolition of the use of animals in science."[2] Additionally, animal rights activists seek to stop people from hunting animals, using animals in the entertainment industry, and displaying animals in zoos.

A student dissects a frog for biology class. Opponents of dissection have proposed alternatives for teaching anatomy.

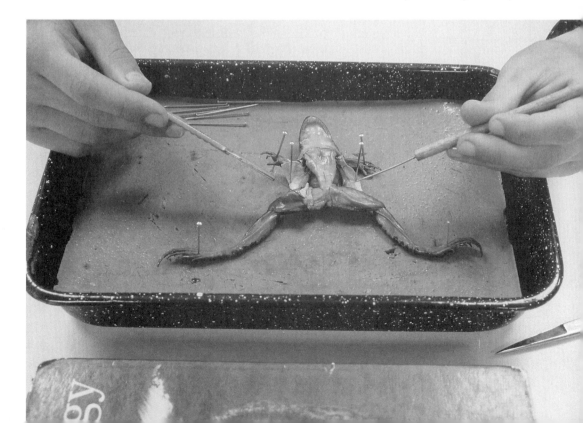

Dissection today

The animal rights movement has generated much interest in animal issues due to its well-publicized protests and campaigns. For instance, Graham's refusal to dissect was supported by many animal rights organizations. Their publicity helped bring the dissection issue to the forefront of the media. Graham's story was broadcast on the news, in the newspapers, and even made into a television special. Due to this publicity Americans learned that animal dissection is common in schools, and many joined efforts to stop this practice.

Americans against dissection in education have supported efforts aimed at changing schools' dissection rules. An example of a program that has received public support is the National Anti-Vivisection Society's (NAVS) Dissection Hotline. Students and parents can call this hotline to learn about dissection in schools and to be advised of their legal rights if the students do not want to dissect.

The NAVS hotline and other efforts have resulted in teachers changing their dissection policies. The National Association of Biology Teachers (NABT) updated its guidance on dissection and alternatives in 1995. The NABT continues to support dissection as a learning tool, but now accepts alternatives in certain situations. The NABT Web site states:

> When the teacher determines that the most effective means to meet the objectives of the class do not require dissection, NABT accepts the use of alternatives to dissection including models and the various forms of multimedia. The Association encourages teachers to be sensitive to substantive student objections to dissection and to consider providing appropriate lessons for those students where necessary.[3]

Dissection alternatives

Dissection alternatives, such as computer software and laboratory kits, are intended to teach biology lessons that are typically learned during dissection. Software allows students to do interactive dissections on the computer. In September 2003 sixteen-year-old Kenwood High School student

3 1833 04736 9951

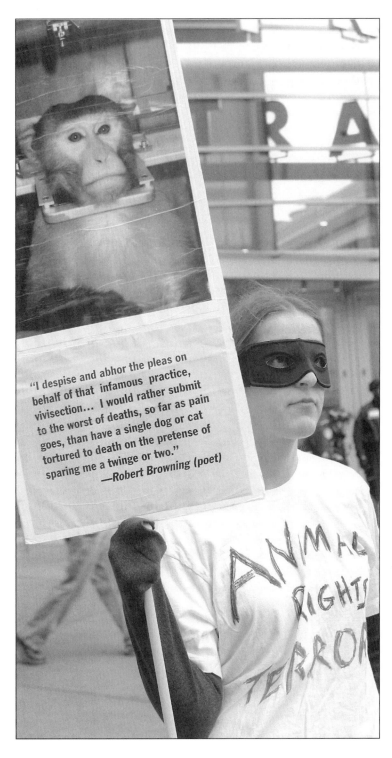

"I despise and abhor the pleas on behalf of that infamous practice, vivisection... I would rather submit to the worst of deaths, so far as pain goes, than have a single dog or cat tortured to death on the pretense of sparing me a twinge or two."
—Robert Browning (poet)

An activist with the Northwest Animal Rights Network marches for animal rights in 2003. Whether animals have rights is hotly debated.

Jennifer Watson refused to dissect a cat in her anatomy class. Unlike Graham, Watson was allowed to complete an alternative assignment, using computer software to simulate the dissection.

Another alternative to dissection is the CellServ laboratory kit. CellServ is a kit, made for beginning high school and college biology classes, that teaches biology through four experiments using cell cultures from humans. The kit was designed to replace animals as tools for teaching biology concepts.

Alternatives have continued to become more common as states have enacted laws that guarantee students the right to choose whether they want to dissect. Nine states, including Graham's state of California, have enacted choice laws or policies. These allow kindergarten through high school students to complete alternative work in science if they oppose dissection.

Animal rights support

These policies and laws have changed because campaigns against dissection have received a good amount of public support. Other animal rights causes, such as abolishing the use of animals as food, as clothing, and in medical research, are more controversial. These causes receive opposition because the majority of people benefit from these uses of animals. Animal rights activists counter that any use of animals, even if it benefits humans, is immoral because it violates animals' rights. However, there is much disagreement as to whether or not animals have rights and, if animals do have rights, what these rights are.

1

Do Animals Have Rights?

THROUGHOUT HISTORY HUMANS have used animals in ways ranging from hunting them for food to using them for entertainment. People have used animals for their own benefit because many believe that the purpose of animals is to serve humans. This belief is based on various religious, philosophical, and scientific viewpoints.

Historically, people have seen animals as a form of entertainment. In A.D. 72 Roman emperor Vespasian ordered the building of the Roman colosseum. At its grand opening in A.D. 80, thousands of animals and gladiators were killed in games while spectators watched. The slaughter of animals, including elephants, lions, and panthers, continued as a way of entertaining colosseum audiences until the sixth century.

For thousands of years, people have used animals for food and clothing. In the 1600s, Europeans established colonies in North America and, needing food and clothing to survive, hunted America's wild animals. Before Europeans came to North America, there were an estimated 30 to 70 million buffalo roaming its lands. By the late 1800s approximately fifteen hundred remained. For many, the belief that animals were placed on the earth for people to use justified the killing of buffalo. This view was widely accepted by Americans because it was supported by their religions.

Religious views

Religions have affected how people around the world view animals. As an example, the teachings of major Asian religions such as Buddhism, Hinduism, and Jainism say that it is wrong for man to harm animals. Followers of Hinduism and Buddhism are taught that when a person dies, his or her soul is reborn into another living creature, which could be an animal or a human. For this reason many Hindus and Buddhists believe that they should treat animals kindly since they could one day be animals themselves. Buddhism also teaches its followers that to live rightly, a person should not kill any living creature. Jains believe that humans should not cause harm to any living creatures because, if they do, their own souls may not attain peace after death.

As this painting depicts, the ancient Romans killed wild animals in the colosseum for entertainment.

These beliefs have affected how followers of these religions treat animals. Many strict Buddhists, Jains, and Hindus are vegetarians because they believe it is wrong to kill a living creature even for food. Most Asian countries have a higher percentage of vegetarians than North American or European countries, where Christianity and Judaism are the predominant religions. For instance, in India an estimated 15 to 20 percent of its citizens are vegetarians as opposed to about 1 percent in the United States.

Western religions

Early European and American beliefs about animals, however, were rooted in the teachings of Christianity and Judaism. Christianity and Judaism's scripture teaches that humans are superior to animals and that animals are made solely for human use. In Genesis, a book in the Old Testament of the Bible that is holy to both Christians and Jews, God directs humans to take control over the animals: "Be fruitful and multiply; fill the earth, and subdue it; have dominion over the fish of the sea, over the birds of the air, and over every living thing that moves on the earth."[4]

Leaders of the Christian church reinforced this belief throughout early European history. Saint Thomas Aquinas, a church leader during the thirteenth century, maintained that only humans, not animals, had souls. Aquinas preached that animals could not reason and make their own decisions. Based on these beliefs, he taught that humans were meant to direct animals' actions.

Care for animals

Other Christian leaders believed that because man was superior to animals, man had a duty to care for them. Saint Francis of Assisi, a friar born in 1182 in Assisi, Italy, taught people that they were responsible for protecting animals and treating them kindly. He preached that all animals were the most obedient of God's creation and deserved humane treatment by man. Saint Francis's dedication to animals resulted in his becoming the patron saint of animals.

Saint Francis's teaching has continued to influence people after his death. His followers honor animals yearly at a Blessing of the Animals. For many years, on the Sunday closest to October 4, people have honored Saint Francis by bringing their pets to the ceremony to be blessed by church leaders.

Early philosophies

Although there were people who shared Saint Francis's belief that man should care for animals, neither the general population nor religious leaders of his time believed that animals had rights or were as worthy as humans. Philosophers also supported the view that animals were meant to serve humans.

Aristotle, a Greek philosopher born in 384 B.C., claimed that animals existed for man's use. He believed that there was a hierarchy of living beings, with humans superior to animals, and animals superior to plants. According to Aristotle,

> We may infer that, after the birth of animals, plants exist for their sake, and that the other animals exist for the sake of man, the tame for use and food, the wild, if not all, at least the greater part of them, for food, and for the provision of clothing and various instruments. Now if nature makes nothing incomplete, and nothing in vain, the inference must be that she has made all animals for the sake of man.[5]

In the following centuries philosophers continued to adopt the idea that animals are inferior to humans. René Descartes, a French philosopher and scientist of the seventeenth century, believed that animals could not think or experience emotions. He likened animals to machines, incapable of feeling and without consciousness. For that reason, he concluded, they did not have rights. For many years, scientists with a growing interest in physiology, the biological study of the functions of living organisms and their parts, used this view to justify their experiments on animals. The animals were often alive and conscious while being cut open and studied.

Immanuel Kant, an eighteenth-century German philosopher, taught that animals were a means to an end for hu-

mans and therefore humans had no duties to animals. It was not until the human rights philosophy was accepted by the general public that philosophers reconsidered their views of animals.

A Catholic priest blesses pets in honor of Saint Francis of Assisi, who taught that animals deserve humane treatment.

Changing viewpoints

Human rights, the idea that all people are born with certain rights, gained widespread acceptance in the 1700s. Europeans and Americans, believing that all humans had the right to life, liberty, and the pursuit of happiness, instituted laws to protect these rights.

Following the general acceptance of human rights, philosophers began to consider whether or not animals, like humans, possessed inherent rights. Henry Salt, an English humanitarian devoted to the promotion of human welfare and to social reforms, wrote *Animal Rights* in 1892. He was among the first to write that animals were guaranteed certain rights. His writings supported the idea that animals should be protected from being abused by humans. For example, Salt, a vegetarian, believed that killing animals for food was a form of abuse.

Jeremy Bentham, a nineteenth-century English philosopher, also advocated the idea that animals should not suffer because of humans. Bentham did not think that an animal's ability or inability to reason should determine its rights. Bentham pointed out that a full-grown horse had more reason than a newborn baby, yet few would argue that a horse has more rights than a baby.

Naturalist Charles Darwin determined that animals suffer pain. His findings led people to protest vivisection.

Bentham claimed that an animal's capacity to suffer is the most important factor in considering how animals should be treated and whether or not they have rights. According to Bentham, "The question is not, Can they reason? Can they talk? But, Can they suffer?"[6]

Scientific findings

Scientific discoveries during the nineteenth century supported Bentham's belief that animals could suffer. Charles Darwin, an English naturalist, published *The Descent of Man* in 1871. In this publication Darwin stated that humans and animals were linked in the evolutionary chain and thus shared similar biology. Based on this, Darwin concluded that animals, like humans, were sensory. Sensory beings are able to experience physical feelings, including pain.

As a result of Darwin's finding, people became more concerned about the pain humans inflict on animals. Specifically, people focused on animal use in scientific experiments. During the nineteenth century, scientists commonly vivisected animals as part of their research. Vivisection is the practice of operating on fully conscious animals as a way to learn about animals' biology. This helped scientists to better understand human biological functions and allowed them to test medical procedures. People became concerned about the pain that animals endured during these experiments. To stop these animals' suffering, people formed groups, such as the New England Anti-Vivisection Society, that called for an end to vivisection.

Animal welfare movement

In addition to protests against vivisection, people organized efforts to improve treatment of animals in other areas. These efforts were the beginning of the animal welfare movement, which is still in force today. The animal welfare movement's goal is to minimize the suffering people inflict on animals. Supporters of this movement believe that people may use animals when necessary, but that people must treat these animals kindly.

The earliest animal welfare organization was established in England in 1824. The mission of the Royal Society for the Prevention of Cruelty to Animals (RSPCA) is to prevent cruelty to animals and promote kindness to animals by enforcing legislation and establishing new laws to protect animals in Great Britain. Efforts of the RSPCA and other animal welfare organizations resulted in the English Parliament passing the Protection of Animals Act in 1911. This law states that it is an offense to subject an animal to unnecessary suffering. The RSPCA remains active, working to establish more animal welfare laws and policies in Great Britain.

In 1866 the first private humane organization was chartered in the United States. The American Society for the Prevention of Cruelty to Animals (ASPCA) was established with the mission to pass anticruelty laws to protect animals in the United States. Continued efforts by animal welfare organizations such as the ASPCA led to the passage of the Animal Welfare Act (AWA) of 1966.

Animal Welfare Act

The AWA sets the standards for the handling, housing, feeding, and caring of animals in laboratories, zoos, circuses, and pet stores, but not for those raised on farms, including fur farms, where animals such as mink are raised to make fur coats. The AWA covers warm-blooded animals such as cats, dogs, nonhuman primates, hamsters, guinea pigs, and rabbits, but not mice, rats, and birds. Examples of the AWA's specific regulations are that laboratories must consult with a veterinarian about how to minimize animals' pain when conducting experiments, and that great apes over fifty-five pounds must be housed in at least a twenty-five-square-foot cage. The U.S. Department of Agriculture (USDA) ensures these specifications are met by inspecting the facilities.

Birth of the animal rights movement

In the 1970s the animal rights movement spun off from the animal welfare movement. While both movements

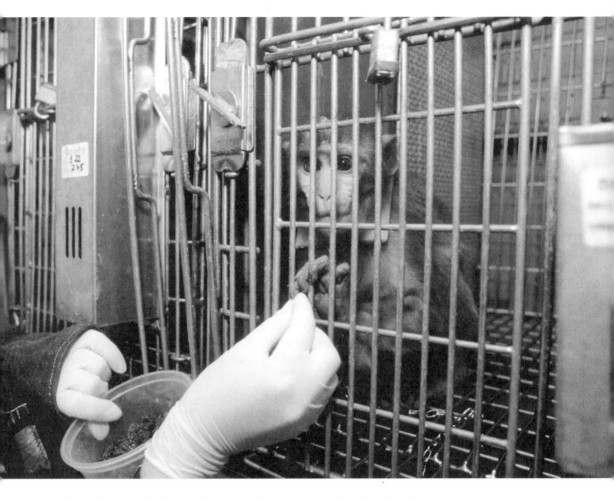

share the goal of stopping cruel treatment of animals, the animal rights movement seeks to end all human interference in the lives of animals.

"Concern for protecting animal welfare was eclipsed by the philosophical imperative that animals, like humans, possess certain fundamental and inalienable rights, and therefore should be treated as moral equals,"[7] writes Harold D. Guither, author of *Animal Rights: History and Scope of a Radical Social Movement*. Animal rights activists believe that animals are born with the right not to be used by humans in any way that does not benefit animals. They also believe that an animal's life is just as worthy as a human life.

A lab technician feeds a monkey used for medical experiments. Many people believe such experimentation violates an animal's rights.

Peter Singer, an Australian professor of philosophy and considered by many the founder of the modern animal rights movement, advocates that when making decisions concerning animals, humans should consider an animal life as important as a human life. Singer believes in utilitarianism, which teaches that when making decisions people must determine the best total outcome for everyone involved, including animals. To Singer, this means that it is wrong to kill animals in medical research because the harm inflicted on animals is greater than the benefit to humans. However, he has stated that some forms of animal experimentation could be justified if it resulted in curing a major human disease.

Growth of the animal rights movement

Tom Regan, an American philosophy professor, agrees with Singer that animals should be given equal consideration. However, Regan writes that all animal use by humans is immoral no matter what the outcome. His 1983 book, *The Case for Animal Rights,* expresses his belief that animals are born with the same inherent value as humans. For this reason he believes that people must treat animals with the same respect that people have for human life. If people believe it is wrong to kill another person for food, clothing, or scientific research, then, according to Regan, it is wrong to kill animals for the same purposes.

Based on both Regan's and Singer's beliefs, numerous animal rights organizations have emerged with missions to establish and protect animals' rights. Among the most well known of these organizations is People for the Ethical Treatment of Animals (PETA).

Ingrid Newkirk and Alex Pacheco founded PETA in 1980 after Newkirk read Singer's *Animal Liberation.* PETA's mission is to stop all use of animals by humans that does not benefit animals. With over 750,000 members and an annual budget exceeding $13 million, PETA has succeeded in achieving major accomplishments. For instance, it persuaded McDonald's, Burger King, and Wendy's to ensure that the animals they use are slaughtered humanely and receive good treatment during their lifetimes.

Today's findings

Members of animal rights organizations generally believe that animals are sentient beings with the ability to communicate, reason, and feel emotion. Recent animal studies support the idea that animals are closely linked to humans in these ways. Therefore, some say animals deserve the same rights as humans.

Studies of Koko, a three-hundred-pound gorilla at the Gorilla Foundation in Northern California, show that she can both communicate and reason. Through sign language, Koko, who has been taught over one thousand signs, is able to communicate with humans. Also, based on intelligence quotient (IQ) tests, which typically are used to determine a person's intelligence and reasoning skills, her IQ

Koko the gorilla uses sign language to communicate with her trainer. Koko has shown that some animals have simple reasoning skills.

has been estimated to be between seventy to ninety-five points. This score is not far below the average human IQ of one hundred. Some say Koko's score refutes the older views of philosophers, such as Descartes, that animals cannot reason.

Studies have shown that in addition to being able to communicate through sign language, animals can understand people's nonverbal cues, such as gestures and looks, and use their own gestures to communicate in response. Adam Miklosi, a researcher at Eötvös University in Budapest, Hungary, conducted communication research on dogs. As part of his research, he taught dogs to get a piece of meat by pulling a string. Once the dogs could do this, the researchers attached the string so that even if the dogs pulled they could not get the meat. When this happened, Miklosi explains, "What they did was basically look back at their owners. If you observe this in a human, you would describe it as an asking-for-help gesture."[8] However, critics say that there is no way humans can determine that this gesture meant the dogs were asking for assistance and therefore the experiment does not support the belief that animals can communicate.

Several researchers also claim that animals feel emotions such as fear, jealousy, and grief. For example, elephants often stand next to their dead kin for days and touch their bodies with their trunks. Many researchers have concluded that the elephants' actions are signs of grief. Studies of rats have also shown that animals experience pleasure. Specifically, studies have shown that when rats play, their brains release large amounts of dopamine, a neurochemical associated with pleasure in human beings. However, it is unknown if dopamine works the same way in both humans and animals.

A focus on animals

These findings have led more people to empathize with animals and work to improve their lives. Although most Americans believe it is acceptable for people to use animals for food, clothing, and in medical research, they also believe that animals should be treated humanely and that people are responsible for reducing animals' suffering whenever possible. This view is in line with the beliefs of animal welfare organizations such as the Humane Society of the United States (HSUS). HSUS states, "As the dominant intelligent life on the Earth, humans are accountable as a species. Though we are not opposed to the legitimate and appropriate utilization of animals in the service of human beings, such utilization gives man neither the right nor the license to exploit or abuse any animal in the process."[9]

Despite support for humane treatment, animal rights remains controversial. Many people do not agree that an animal's life is as worthy as a human's. For this reason, topics such as animal experimentation, in which animal lives are sacrificed in research that may save human lives, are passionately debated.

Harold D. Guither, a retired professor of agricultural policy, writes that even though there is much disagreement as to whether animals have rights or not, the animal rights debate will ultimately result in changes in how people treat animals:

> The philosophers and activists do not completely agree on how humans should interact with animals, but all support more humane treatment. These concerns have ignited a social movement that is not likely to go away since the arguments are based on reason, not emotion. If enough people accept these ideas, major changes in the use and treatment of animals will take place.[10]

2

Animals as Food

ANIMALS AND ANIMAL products make up a major part of Americans' diets. Only an estimated 1 to 2 percent of Americans are vegetarians or vegans. Vegetarians are people who do not eat any meat products, including beef, pork, chicken, and seafood, while vegans do not eat meat or any animal products, including eggs and dairy. The remaining 98 to 99 percent of Americans consume meat, eggs, and dairy in great quantities.

According to the U.S. Department of Agriculture (USDA), a typical American annually consumes 64 pounds of beef, 47.8 pounds of pork, 52 pounds of chicken, and 14.5 pounds of seafood. Additionally, an average person in the United States eats from 234 to 244 eggs each year and 580 pounds of dairy products, which include milk, cheese, and other milk-based products.

Americans eat meat and other animal products not only because they like the taste but also because these foods meet daily nutritional needs. The USDA recommends that people eat two to three servings of protein daily. The majority of protein choices are animals or animal products such as beef, poultry, fish, and eggs. The USDA also recommends two to three servings from the dairy group, including milk, yogurt, and cheese.

In recent years Americans have become concerned with how the animals they eat are handled and killed and how animals that produce products such as eggs are treated. Animal welfare groups and animal rights organizations have conducted publicity campaigns, explicitly describing how they say farm animals are raised and slaughtered, and voicing their concern about the welfare of animals raised on farms. Farmers today strive to balance the needs and wants of the American diet with calls for ethical treatment of animals. The American Meat Institute (AMI), the United States' oldest and largest meat and poultry trade association, encourages its members to treat their animals humanely and states, "The vast majority of Americans choose to consume meat and poultry and rightfully expect

Many people enjoy eating hamburgers. Ninety-eight percent of Americans eat meat.

that these products are derived from animals that are handled humanely."[11]

Intensive farms

Before World War II, small-scale, family-owned farms were common. On these farms chickens, cows, and pigs roamed in fenced areas and were fed and cared for by a farmer and his family. In the latter twentieth century, farming changed.

The majority of today's U.S. farms are large-scale, "intensive" farms. These are characterized by less human-animal interaction and significantly more livestock than small-scale

These turkeys live in crowded conditions on an intensive farm. Some people believe such farms are inhumane and unethical.

farms. Intensive farms use confined housing, where animals are kept in cages or stalls indoors, and automation, where jobs that people used to do, such as feeding the animals, are replaced by mechanical means. Confined housing and automation are ways to reduce the cost of raising large numbers of animals as well as to prevent animals from harming or spreading disease to one another.

Intensive farm housing

On intensive farms housing varies depending on the type of animal. For example, veal calves are placed in separate stalls a few days after birth. They remain in these stalls until they are slaughtered eighteen to twenty weeks later. Normally the calves are tethered around their necks to keep them confined to their stalls. The tethered veal calves can lie down, stand, move a few feet back and forward, but cannot turn around.

Dairy cows are also frequently tethered in stalls. However, 25 percent of dairy cows are in "free stalls," which they can leave and enter at will. Beef cattle have more room than dairy cows, as they are often raised in feedlots, confined yards with watering and feeding facilities.

Chickens are confined to pens or litters, large rooms with litter spread on the floors, depending on what the chickens' purpose is. Layers, hens that are used to produce eggs, are raised in small groups in cages. These cages are stacked in tiers and lined in rows, with forty thousand to one hundred thousand chickens per house. Broilers, chickens raised to be slaughtered and sold as poultry, are raised on litter in houses of twenty thousand birds.

Intensive-farm owners believe that confining animals is better for the health of their animals than allowing them to roam. For example, keeping cows in separate stalls reduces the chance of disease being spread from one animal to another. According to a report by Carolyn Stull of the University of California at Davis, Richard Warner of Cornell University, and Lowell Wilson of Pennsylvania State University, "In a study comparing individual stalls with pens containing up to 50 calves, more health-related problems were observed in the group-rearing situations. A significantly higher morbidity was experienced in calves housed in group pens, with enteric and respiratory diseases as the most common causes."[12]

Additionally, farmers claim that separate stalls reduce fights among animals. The stalls separate aggressive young bulls, eliminating the possibility of fights that would harm them. Likewise, farmers believe that housing chickens in cages protects the birds from fights during feeding times and also ensures that each bird gets the proper amount of food. Farmers point out that when large groups of chickens are housed together and have room to roam, the chickens often peck at each other during feeding time in an attempt to get their fair share of food. By confining chickens to small groups in cages, farmers can ensure that each bird is well fed and fighting does not occur.

Concerns with housing

Even though confined housing helps reduce fights and disease and ensures that all animals receive their food, animal advocates have several concerns about animals' confinement. One is the effect of lack of space on the animals. A chicken's wingspan is thirty-two inches, but its cage can be as little as twenty inches wide. This gives the chicken no room to spread its wings, which is one of its natural instincts. Animal rights advocates are concerned that this causes stress to the chickens. Additionally, because chickens have limited space to walk, many develop chronic leg pain, swollen joints, brittle bones, and arthritis.

While intensive farmers claim that confinement keeps their animals physically healthy, critics of confined housing charge that it hurts animals' emotional well-being. For instance, boredom and frustration may result from confinement. The animals often live their lives in a cage or a stall indoors, never having the opportunity to roam as they would in their natural habitat. Tom Regan believes that this results in not only physical but also emotional problems for farm animals such as veal calves. "Veal calves suffer, both physically and psychologically," Regan writes. "Psychologically, they suffer because their life of solitary confinement

is characterized by abject deprivation. Throughout their lives they are denied the opportunity to suckle and graze, denied the opportunity to stretch their legs, and denied the fresh air and sunlight they naturally enjoy."[13]

Some dairy cows receive hormones to make them produce more milk, but the hormones may also cause painful diseases.

Producing desired products

Farmers place their animals on special diets to help them produce either high quality meats or great quantities of animal products. For example, to ensure that veal meat is healthy, tender, and white, which is preferred by consumers, farmers carefully oversee their veal calves' diet. Veal calves are not permitted to suckle their mothers' milk. Instead, they receive a milk replacer diet for the eighteen to twenty weeks before they are slaughtered.

The milk replacer diet is composed of dairy products including skim milk, whey, and sweet buttermilk cream with water. Proteins, minerals, and vitamins are also added. The diet is low in iron to ensure that the veal meat is white, but because a depletion of iron leads to a lack of appetite, farmers provide the veal calves with some iron so that they eat enough to reach the desired weight, three hundred to four hundred pounds, at slaughter.

Because of the lack of iron in their diet, many veal calves experience frequent diarrhea and are chronically anemic, meaning the calves have less than the normal number of red blood cells in their blood. Critics claim that restricting iron in the calves' diet is cruel because anemia can result in chronic weakness and fatigue. Some calves have been observed licking their metal crates in order to obtain the iron.

In addition to keeping animals on special diets, farmers give them hormones that increase their production of animal products. In the United States 25 percent of dairy farmers give recombinant bovine somatotropin (BST) to their dairy cows. BST causes a dairy cow to produce 10 to 25 percent more milk than it would naturally. BST concerns people who say it has detrimental effects on dairy cows. The European Union (EU), a union of twenty-five European countries that determines joint economic and political decisions for all the countries, prohibits the use of BST, based on a report from their Scientific Committee on Animal Health and Animal Welfare. The report claims that BST may cause dairy cows to experience lameness, a condition in which walking causes pain, or mastitis, a painful inflammation of the cow's udder.

Common practices

Besides controlling animals' housing and diets, farmers use other methods to keep their animals safe and healthy. One method is to trim the beaks of their egg-laying chickens. In beak trimming, a chicken's beak is seared off with a hot wire. The blade both melts and cuts through the beak.

Farmers practice beak trimming because it has been shown to prevent feather pecking and cannibalism that can occur within a group of chickens. With their beaks intact, chickens that get into fights can cause pain and injury to one another. They can pluck each other's feathers out and sometimes even peck each other to death and then eat the remains.

However, studies have shown that although beak trimming prevents feather pecking and cannibalism, it may also result in pain. According to Ian J.H. Duncan, a professor of poultry science at the University of Guelph, Ontario, the tip of a chicken's beak has pain receptors, and he believes this means that cutting and heating the beak causes acute pain. Additionally, it has been shown that as the nerve fibers in the stump of a chicken's beak start to regenerate, neuromas, tangled nerve masses that cause phantom limb pain in human beings after a limb has been amputated, also form. This could result in chickens experiencing the same phantom pain that people experience after a limb amputation.

A widespread and longstanding method used by farmers to keep their cows healthy is to dock cows' tails. To dock a cow's tail, a farmer places a tight rubber ring around the lower part of a cow's tail and then removes the portion of the tail below the ring. Farmers use tail docking because it helps keep the cows clean, and some believe that it also reduces the transmission of disease. Cows sometimes defecate directly onto their tails, and tail movements can then splatter feces and other material onto the cow's body. Some farmers believe that the transfer of feces onto the udder, where a cow's milk is stored, can lead to disease and may potentially prevent the cow from producing milk.

Critics of tail docking charge that it is unnecessary and point to several studies supporting their claim. The *Animal Welfare Information Center Bulletin* reported one study that concluded that cows with docked tails were not cleaner or in better udder health than cows without docked tails. The study was conducted on a commercial free-stall dairy farm in British Columbia. For eight weeks, the farmer left the tails of about half of his five hundred milk cows intact and docked the other half. "During this time, we compared cow cleanliness, udder cleanliness, and udder health.

We found no difference between cows with intact tails and those that had been docked, in terms of any of our cleanliness measures, somatic cell counts (a measure of udder health), or cases of mastitis as diagnosed by the herd veterinarian,"[14] write C.B. Tucker and D.M. Weary of the experiment.

Animal slaughter

People are concerned with not only how animals are treated on farms but also how these animals are slaughtered. In 1999, 4 million sheep, 23 million ducks, 38 million cattle, 102 million pigs, and 8 billion chickens were slaughtered for food in the United States. Until the late 1950s painful methods were used to slaughter animals. An example of one of these methods was to slit an animal's throat while the animal was still conscious. People began to voice their concerns about these methods, and their concern resulted in the Humane Slaughter Act of 1958.

The Humane Slaughter Act requires that animals be rendered unconscious before they are slaughtered. A slaughterhouse often stuns farm animals by either using an electric shock or shooting a retractable bolt into the animal's forehead to knock it out. Then the animals are moved down a conveyor belt to be butchered and skinned.

There are several concerns about current slaughterhouse practices. One concern is that, due to stunning failures, animals are slaughtered while fully conscious. In 1996 the USDA hired Temple Grandin, an animal scientist at Colorado State University, to inspect two dozen meat-processing plants across the nation. Grandin discovered several problems with slaughtering methods.

To stun the cows and pigs before slaughter, the meat plant workers shot retractable bolts into the brains of cows and pigs. At two-thirds of the beef plants and at one-third of the pork plants she inspected, Grandin realized that the bolt guns were either not working or not being used correctly. She saw cows and pigs that were still conscious as they moved down the line to be skinned.

Public response to intensive farming

Animal rights activists have responded to what they call the inhumane care and slaughter of farm animals by trying to abolish the use of animals in agriculture. To accomplish this, activists have initiated campaigns aimed at stopping people from eating meat and animal products. An example of an animal rights effort is the annual "Great American Meatout" sponsored by Farm Animal Reform Movement (FARM). Once a year, FARM solicits people to give up meat for a day or longer. Celebrities such as Ally Sheedy and Doris Day have supported this effort.

However, there is more public support for improving farm animal treatment rather than abolishing animal use. For example, consumers have supported the growth of the free-range egg and poultry market. Free-range, or natural, poultry eggs come from chickens that are allowed to roam outside for part of the day. People who buy these products

Colorado animal scientist Temple Grandin found inhumane practices in many U.S. slaughterhouses in 1996.

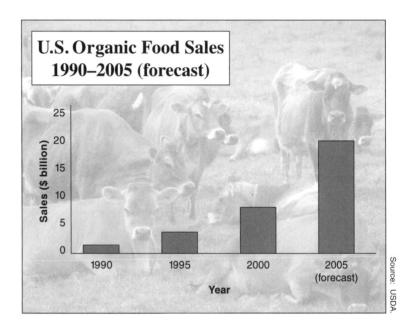

U.S. Organic Food Sales 1990–2005 (forecast)

Source: USDA.

believe that the chickens live less stressful lives than those that are confined all the time. People who are concerned with the detrimental effects of BST and other chemicals buy only organic foods, a term for food from animals raised without being given food additives or chemicals. The *Natural Business Journal* estimates that natural and organic poultry, meat, and fish accounted for 6 percent of the U.S. market in 2002, a 25 percent rise from previous years.

Farmers' response

In part because the public has voiced concern about the treatment of farm animals, farmers have taken an active approach to addressing animal welfare issues. Several farm industry organizations have funded research to better understand the behavioral and psychological needs of livestock so that they can better meet these needs. For example, the American Meat Institute (AMI) helped fund and organize the 2004 International Meat Animal Welfare Conference. This conference was held in response to the growing interest in animal welfare and provided its attendees information about the latest research in animal handling and welfare during livestock production, transport, and processing.

In addition to funding research, farm industry professionals attend classes to learn more about the needs of their animals. In 2003 farmers, slaughterhouse managers, and animal transport drivers attended classes such as "Creating an Animal Welfare Mindset in Your Company" and "Humane Turkey Production" sponsored by the AMI.

Because the Animal Welfare Act does not apply to animals on farms, professional farming associations have taken the initiative to develop their own animal welfare regulations based on farm animal research and studies, animal welfare classes, and their own professional experience. An example of a recent effort is the 2003 edition of the United Egg Producers' *Animal Husbandry Guidelines, Overview of Best Managing Practices for U.S. Egg Laying Flocks.* This document gives regulations for chicken care, including the feeding and housing of the animals. Specific regulations include that birds housed in cages must have ready access to feed troughs directly in front of their cages, that water is accessed easily from each cage, and that the chickens' housing must include standby generators to supply emergency power for lighting, watering, ventilation, feeding, and egg collection.

As public interest in the welfare of farm animals grows, it is likely that farming organizations will continue to address the needs of their animals. According to Ken Klippen, a vice president of United Egg Producers, a trade group based in Alpharetta, Georgia, "Customers used to tell us what they wanted to eat. Now they tell us how they want it produced."[15]

3

Animals in Science

In SEPTEMBER 2001 the Coulston Foundation's White Sands Research Center in Alamogordo, New Mexico, was set on fire. The fire severely damaged the laboratory, causing a million dollars' worth of damage to the building and equipment, while animals and humans were not harmed. The White Sands Research Center is a not-for-profit biomedical research laboratory that conducts research on chimpanzees to confirm the safety of new vaccines for humans. The Animal Liberation Foundation (ALF), an extremist animal rights group, claimed responsibility for the fire. They, like most animal rights organizations, believe that experiments using animals are immoral.

Animal research is a highly charged issue because both animal and human lives are at stake. Each year millions of animals die in labs as a result of research projects, while millions of human lives are saved by the vaccines, medications, and medical procedures that are developed due to this animal research.

Research animals

According to the U.S. Department of Agriculture (USDA), in 2001 approximately 1.2 million animals were used in U.S. research. These numbers are based on the required reports that laboratories submit to the USDA. However, laboratories only submit numbers for animals covered under the Animal Welfare Act, which does not include mice, rats, birds, and fish. According to the Center for Laboratory Animal Welfare, approximately 95 percent of the animals used in research are rats and mice. This equates to approximately 25 million animals used annually in U.S. laboratories. Worldwide approximately 100 million animals per year undergo laboratory testing.

The animals used in laboratories come from two main sources—pounds and breeders. In pound seizure, dealers collect unwanted animals from shelters or pounds and sell them to laboratories. While fourteen states prohibit pound seizure, five states require that pounds and shelters give their unwanted animals to dealers who sell them to research facilities. These five states claim that because the unwanted animals would otherwise be euthanized, it is better to use them in experiments that may benefit humans.

Other ways for research facilities to obtain animals is to breed them or purchase them from laboratories that breed animals. With fifty-four facilities in fifteen countries, Charles River Laboratories of Wilmington, Massachusetts, is the world's largest producer of animals bred for research. Many research facilities purchase their animals from them.

Animal Research

Animals used for research in 2001 and some of the benefits:

	Primates 49,382	AIDS, cancer, Alzheimer's disease, drug addiction, cardiovascular disease research, and vaccine development
	Rats, mice 20–25 mil.	Breast cancer research, cancer drug development, gene therapy for cystic fibrosis, studies of multiple sclerosis, and Lou Gehrig's disease
	Pigs 60,353	Diabetes research, development of laproscopic surgical techniques

Source: Americans for Medical Progress.

These rhesus monkeys are members of a population raised by a scientific laboratory specifically for experimental use.

Types of experiments

Animals are used in three major types of research: product testing, education, and biomedical research. Biomedical research is the most common purpose for animal experiments. About 87 percent of lab animals are used in biomedical research. Biomedical research includes evaluating the safety and effectiveness of drugs and vaccines and conducting experiments to determine how the body works and is affected by disease.

In biomedical research in North Carolina, for example, scientists led by Miguel Nicolelis of Duke University built a brain implant that is meant to allow humans to eventually control robotic arms with their thoughts. The scientists achieved initial success with two monkeys. Implants were placed in two monkeys' brains, and wires ran out of them down to robotic arms. Eventually the monkeys were able to use their thoughts to control the arms. This technology could lead to enabling paralyzed people to operate machines or tools with their thoughts.

Reasons for animal use

Animals are used in scientific research because their biology is similar to humans'. Scientists and researchers can study both the short-term and long-term effects of new medicines, procedures, and vaccines on animals. From these results, scientists determine the potential effects of the medicines, procedures, and vaccines on humans.

There is a long history of breakthrough medical developments resulting from animal research. For example, in the summer of 1952 more than fifty-eight thousand American children contracted polio. Polio killed thousands of these children and left thousands of others paralyzed. Due to animal testing a safe polio vaccine was developed. By the end of the decade the number of polio cases in the United States had been reduced to twelve. "[The polio vaccine's] impact has been global," writes Carl Cohen, coauthor of *The Animal Rights Debate*. "How many have been spared misery and death by this one great step in medical science we can hardly guess. But about this wonderful vaccine and its successors we do know one thing for certain: It could not have been achieved without the use of laboratory animals."[16]

By experimenting on animals, scientists achieved similar successes throughout the twentieth century. Of the seventy-six Nobel prizes awarded in medicine or physiology during the twentieth century, fifty-four of the awards were for studies based on animal research. Examples of these studies' findings include the development of insulin, which is used to treat diabetes, and the discovery that cholesterol is linked to heart disease.

Research today

Currently, many animals are being used in the fight against the disease AIDS (acquired immune deficiency syndrome) and HIV (human immune deficiency virus), a virus that develops into AIDS. This disease has killed millions of people worldwide. In 2003 approximately 40 million people around the globe were affected with HIV or AIDS. During this same year, there were 3 million deaths from AIDS.

Animal testing has played an active role in the development of drugs and treatments used to combat HIV. For example, animals were used to help test Tenofovir, a Food and Drug Administration–approved drug that prevents HIV from reproducing in uninfected cells. Additionally, monkeys are a part of the effort to find a vaccine to prevent humans from contracting AIDS. An antiviral drug called PMPA that prevents infection by the Simian immunodeficiency virus (SIV), a virus similar to HIV that affects monkeys, was developed through research on monkeys and has provided leads in the search for an HIV vaccine.

AIDS and HIV affect so many human lives that even some who advocate animal rights believe that animals should be used in this research. Melissa Etheridge, a popular singer who once gave her support to PETA (People for the Ethical Treatment of Animals) by appearing in an anti-fur ad, made a decision not to do any more visible work for PETA because of its stance on AIDS and HIV testing. Etheridge disagrees with PETA's fight against the use of animals in all research, including HIV and AIDS research. "My father died of cancer, and I've lost too many friends to AIDS," Etheridge explains. "So I do believe in animals losing their lives to eradicate cancer and AIDS from our lives; I believe in that."[17]

Impact of regulations

To ensure that animals used in this research are treated as humanely as possible and that their suffering is eliminated or reduced, most lab animals are treated in accordance with the Animal Welfare Act (AWA). The AWA

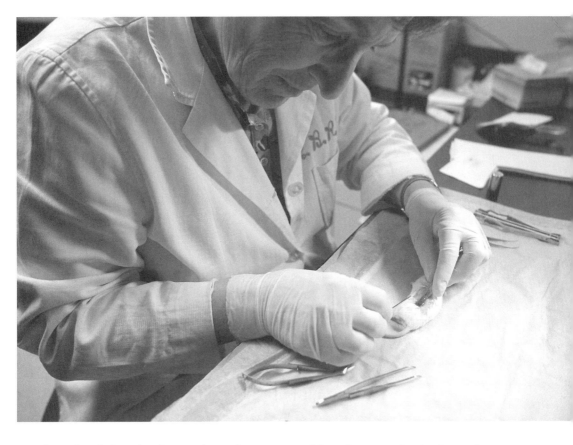

requires that lab animals receive adequate nutrition, housing, and veterinarian care. Since the AWA first became law, amendments have been added extending the requirements. For example, the 1985 AWA amendment mandates exercise for dogs and environmental enrichment for primates, such as providing perches, swings, and mirrors for them to use, to promote their psychological well-being. The 1990 amendment establishes a holding period of at least five days for dogs and cats at shelters and other holding facilities before they can be sent to research laboratories.

Each research facility is required to obtain a permit from the USDA, which enforces the AWA, in order to conduct research on animals. Once they receive their permits, the facilities must submit to inspections by the USDA's Animal and Plant Health Inspection Service (APHIS). Additionally, the facilities must submit reports annually to the

A scientist conducts AIDS research on a mouse. Animal testing has played a large role in developing AIDS treatments.

USDA to demonstrate that they are following the AWA and reducing animals' suffering as much as possible. If they do not follow these rules, the USDA can take action, such as imposing a fine, against the labs. According to the USDA 2001 Animal Welfare Report to Congress, based on the research laboratories' annual reports, 57 percent of warm-blooded animals covered by the AWA experienced no pain or distress, 34 percent experienced pain that was alleviated, and 8.5 percent experienced unrelieved pain. These numbers remained steady from 1996 to 2001.

Animal research concerns

Animal rights advocates charge that the welfare of laboratory mice and rats, which make up over 95 percent of all animals in laboratories, is neglected because the AWA does not cover these animals. Animal welfare supporters sued the USDA in an effort to include mice and rats in the AWA, but in 2002 President George W. Bush signed the Farm Bill

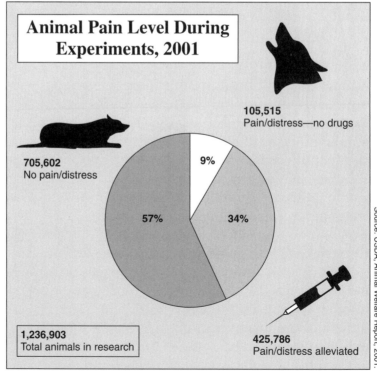

Animal Pain Level During Experiments, 2001

105,515
Pain/distress—no drugs

705,602
No pain/distress

9%

57%

34%

1,236,903
Total animals in research

425,786
Pain/distress alleviated

Source: USDA, Animal Welfare Report, 2001.

into law, which amended the AWA to permanently exclude rats, mice, and birds. The USDA and other AWA supporters counter that the AWA does not need to cover mice and rats because their treatment is overseen by other regulations such as the U.S. Department of Health and Human Services Public Health Service's (PHS) *Policy on Humane Care and Use of Laboratory Animals.*

Examples of the PHS guidelines include that laboratories provide adequate veterinary care for their animals, that housing for animals should allow them easy access to food and water, and that, when possible, social animals should be housed in pairs or groups. Laboratories that receive funding or other support from PHS must follow its PHS animal welfare policy or the laboratories' funding could be revoked.

Although the AWA and PHS have set guidelines to oversee animal care in laboratories, animal rights and animal welfare supporters are concerned that research facilities are able to avoid these rules. Because the USDA is only required by the AWA to inspect research facilities once a year, they claim that research facilities can avoid adhering to the AWA. As an example, critics cite allegations of animal abuse at Columbia University's Institute of Comparative Medicine in 2003.

Veterinarian Cathy Dell'Orto was working at Columbia University as a postdoctoral fellow when she became upset at how some animals in its research laboratory were treated. She was convinced that some of the animals were maltreated and charged that after baboons had their eyeballs removed as part of stroke therapy research, they were left to suffer in their cages rather than being euthanized. After reporting her findings to the university and then to the public via PETA, Dell'Orto left the university.

Prior to Dell'Orto's public allegations, neither the USDA nor Columbia University's Institutional Animal Care and Use Committee (IACUC), a committee established at each research facility to oversee the care of animals used in experiments, had found any problems with Columbia's animal care. Dell'Orto's public allegations led to an investigation by the USDA. After investigating Dell'Orto's claims, the USDA indicated to the Humane Society of the United States (HSUS) that upon inspection it found inadequate training of veterinary staff, poor communication between caretakers and staff, and inadequate observation of animals postoperatively. "The Columbia case illustrates that a clean bill of health from an IACUC or the USDA does not mean that all is well for the animals inside a research institution,"[18] said Martin Stephens, vice president for animal research issues at HSUS, commenting on the fact the USDA did not find the problems during prior inspections.

Another concern of animal activists is the growing interest in scientific procedures such as cloning, a technique to produce genetically identical copies of animals. Farmers are interested in cloning because it could give them the ability to select and propagate the best animals, such as beef cattle that have tender meat and are disease resistant, dairy cows and goats that produce large quantities of milk, and sheep that produce high-quality wool. In 1997 scientists at the Roslin Institute in Edinburgh, Scotland, cloned a sheep by using its genes, which determine an animal's inherited traits. They extracted an egg from a sheep and replaced the egg's genes with genes taken from a second sheep. Then they implanted, or inserted, the altered egg back into the first sheep. As a result, the first sheep gave birth to a lamb, named Dolly, that was identical to the second sheep.

Animal rights advocates claim that cloning is cruel to the animals. According to HSUS, cloned animals have health problems such as respiratory distress, pneumonia, lethargy, and arthritis, an ailment that afflicted Dolly.

Animal rights activism

In the past three decades animal rights activists have voiced their concerns by protesting against animal research facilities and their scientists. Most of these protests have been legal while others, like the arson at the Coulston facility, have been illegal. In the year 2000 the ALF claimed

responsibility for 136 other unlawful actions in addition to the Coulston arson. These actions resulted in more than $1.6 million in damage and the freeing of nearly five thousand animals.

The ALF claims that they are benefiting animals when they break into research facilities, release animals from their cages, and let them outside. In response, research facility professionals charge that this is harmful to the animals. "The majority of these [stolen] animals, particularly the minks and laboratory mice, die from exposure, starvation," says Don McKinney, spokesperson for Coulston. "They get eaten by predators. All [the animal rights activists] have really done is just sign the death warrant for a majority of those animals."[19]

Although many animal rights groups agree with the ALF's goal to stop animal use in research, most disagree

A researcher assesses damage caused by animal rights extremists. The extremists claim their actions benefit animals.

A scientist works with a cell culture. Culture tests can be used as an alternative to animal experimentation.

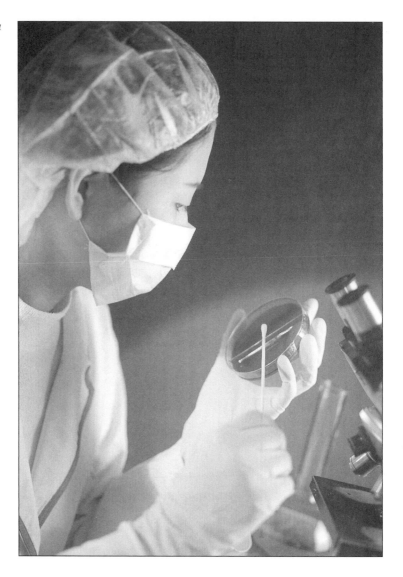

with the ALF's illegal methods. Instead, groups such as PETA campaign against animal research in legal ways such as protesting at facilities and writing letters to U.S. government representatives, calling for the end of animal research.

Alternatives to animal use

Animal research protesters encourage laboratories to use research methods that do not involve animals. They claim that animal testing can be replaced by alternative methods such as computer models. Computer models can simulate biological functions and then test the effects of vaccines and chemicals on these functions. For example, Captopril, a high blood pressure medication, was designed with the help of computer models.

Other alternatives include cell samples and culture tests in which human or bacteria cells are bombarded with diseases and then the results are monitored. An example of a culture test is the "Ames" test, in which a chemical or food additive is tested for its ability to produce mutations in selected strains of bacteria. Positive test results signal the possibility that the substance could cause cancer.

Although the majority of American scientists support the development of alternatives to animal testing, most believe that alternatives cannot replace all animal testing. According to researchers, the alternatives do not take into account the long-term effects of vaccines and medicines on all of the body's systems. For example, cell samples and culture tests are conducted in vitro, outside the body in an artificial environment such as a petri dish or test tube. Although they may test the reaction of one body system, they are independent of other complex biological systems in the body. "Many of the processes that occur within the human body remain too complex to be simulated by a computer or cell culture," according to the National Association of Biomedical Research. "We face too many terrible health problems—like cancer, AIDS, heart disease, Alzheimer's disease, birth defects and mental illness—to eliminate animal research that has been responsible for so many advances in medical use."[20]

Alternative support

Although most scientists do not believe alternatives can replace all animal testing, they are open to using alternatives that they believe will give results as comprehensive as animal tests. Research and medical facilities such as Johns Hopkins University support the study of nonanimal testing and experiments. For example, the Johns Hopkins Center for Alternatives to Animal Testing was formed in 1981 to develop nonanimal biomedical research. In 2001, at a symposium to celebrate the Johns Hopkins Center's twentieth year, Bernard A. Schwetz, a guest speaker from the Food and Drug Administration said, "Our plans in the last 20 years to develop and validate in vitro and alternative tests to reduce our dependence on whole-animal toxicology tests, though not fully realized, are still laudable goals for the future."[21]

Due to the influence of the animal welfare and animal rights efforts, the AWA now requires U.S. research laboratories to implement the "three Rs," a method of reducing the number of animals used in tests and the pain caused to animals. The three Rs stand for replacement, reduction, and refinement of animal testing whenever possible. In replacement, nonanimal techniques are substituted for animal research. Reduction is minimizing the number of animals needed for a certain experiment. Refinement is the modification of a technique to reduce pain to animals.

To enforce the application of the three Rs, the AWA inspectors ask research facilities to provide proof that they have considered the three Rs when planning and conducting animal experiments. The implementation of the three-R method appears to have contributed to the reduction of animal use in experiments. Since 1968, according to Andrew Rowan, a senior vice president at the Humane Society, the annual use of dogs, cats, primates, rabbits, hamsters, and guinea pigs has declined approximately 50 percent.

Animal research, like all animal issues, has received significant attention since the animal rights movement began. Although the animal rights movement has not succeeded in its goal of eliminating all animal use in research, it has fostered greater public interest in animal welfare. This interest has resulted in the development of more alternatives to animal testing as well as regulations that oversee the care of animals used in experiments.

4

Animals in Fashion and Cosmetics

HISTORICALLY PEOPLE HAVE used animal products in an effort to enhance their beauty and to be fashionable. Thousands of years ago the Egyptians made aromatics from animal fat and used them like perfumes of today. Wearing animal furs as coats and hats became popular in Europe as far back as the Middle Ages. In addition to wearing furs for warmth, during the sixteenth century people wore furs such as beaver hats because they were considered stylish. To many people, owning and wearing a fur coat is a symbol of wealth and high fashion.

Today animals remain an integral part of both the clothing and cosmetics industries. Many cosmetics and beauty products are tested on animals to determine the products' safety. In the United States approximately fifty thousand animals per year are used in these tests, with many experiencing pain or dying as a result. In the fur industry over 30 million animals per year are killed for their pelts.

Animal use in these industries is controversial because it harms animals but does not greatly benefit humans. Since the animal rights movement emerged, using animals for vanity's sake has been hotly debated. Campaigns against wearing fur and testing cosmetics on animals have had significant effects on both the fur and cosmetics industries.

The fur industry

Producing and selling fur is a major industry. In 2001, according to the International Fur Trade Federation, worldwide

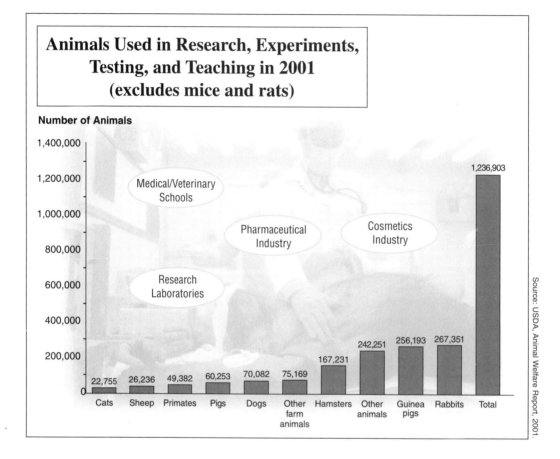

Animals Used in Research, Experiments, Testing, and Teaching in 2001 (excludes mice and rats)

Number of Animals

Medical/Veterinary Schools

Pharmaceutical Industry

Cosmetics Industry

Research Laboratories

Cats	22,755
Sheep	26,236
Primates	49,382
Pigs	60,253
Dogs	70,082
Other farm animals	75,169
Hamsters	167,231
Other animals	242,251
Guinea pigs	256,193
Rabbits	267,351
Total	1,236,903

Source: USDA, Animal Welfare Report, 2001.

sales of fur items totaled approximately $11 billion. Of these furs, the most popular is mink. Several pelts are needed to make one coat or one hat. One forty-inch-long mink coat typically requires sixty mink pelts. For this reason, millions of mink pelts are needed annually to meet consumer demand.

Mink coats and accessories are made from pelts of mink that are either raised on fur farms or caught by trappers. In 2002 fur farms worldwide produced approximately 31 million mink pelts, with 2.6 million of these produced by the 318 fur farms in the United States.

Fur farms

Fur farms are run much like intensive agricultural farms. Fur farmers produce as many healthy animals as possible to meet the demands of the consumers.

On a typical fur farm it takes less than a year to raise and slaughter mink for their pelts. The young, called kits, are vaccinated to prevent health problems such as distemper and botulism and placed in mesh cages. One to four mink live in each cage. The mesh cages are often placed above-ground with a fence surrounding the area to prevent the mink's escape.

After kits molt, or grow their winter fur, they are killed using noninvasive methods, meaning they are not slit with a knife, in order to preserve the pelt. Common methods of slaughter are to euthanize mink with gas or by injection.

Fur-farming regulations

Because the Animal Welfare Act does not apply to animals on fur farms, the fur industry developed its own regulations to ensure that the farmed mink receive proper care and are humanely euthanized. The Fur Commission USA

Farm-raised mink are vaccinated to prevent disease. Animal rights groups are concerned about the treatment of mink on fur farms.

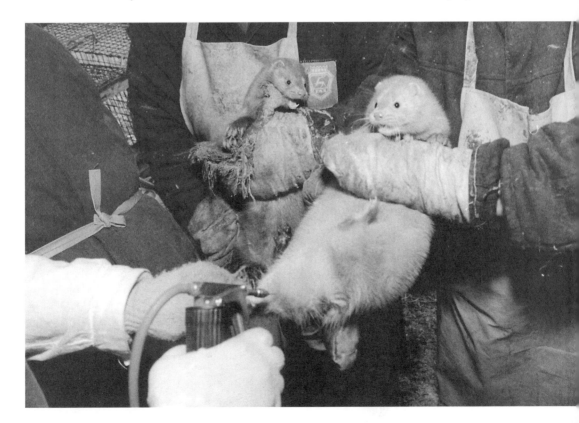

(FCUSA), an association of 420 mink-farming families on 330 farms, has specific standards for animal care that its members must follow. Over 95 percent of U.S. fur-farm owners are members of FCUSA.

To receive a FCUSA certificate of merit fur farmers must abide by the organization's "Standard Guidelines for the Operation of Mink Farms in the United States." The guidelines specify how fur farmers should house their mink, what constitutes adequate nutrition, and when and what type of veterinary care should be given to mink.

Additionally, the FCUSA sets strict standards for the euthanasia of mink, following recommendations of the American Veterinarian Association. FCUSA guidelines stress that its members should use bottled gas to slaughter the kits. This is considered among the least painful of slaughtering methods. Fur farmers following the FCUSA recommendations for slaughter bring a mobile unit to each mink's cage for its euthanasia. This is done because transporting mink to another location for their slaughter typically increases their stress. The mobile unit is an airtight container prefilled with gas. The animal is placed inside and usually dies in less than a minute.

Fur-farming concerns

Animal rights advocates are concerned about the mink's treatment at the farms. Critics contend that even if the mink receive adequate nutrition and care, being raised on a fur farm is unnatural and stressful. Mink are normally nocturnal animals that spend much of their time in the water, but cannot do so on fur farms. "Confined in cages, ranched mink are like fish out of water," writes Tom Regan, coauthor of *The Case for Animal Rights.* "Much of the waking hours finds them pacing, back and forth, back and forth, the boundaries of their diminished life defined by the path they repeat over and over again, in their wire-mesh world."[22]

Fur farmers argue that it is in their best interest not only to treat mink humanely but to keep them content. In order to produce healthy pelts, they go beyond meeting fur-bearing animals' basic needs, they claim. According to Larry Frye, a fur rancher,

> While every good farmer is concerned about the well being of their animals, fur farmers have special concerns about comfort and pampering because of the fact that a fur-bearing animal's health is directly reflected in their coat. Good housekeeping and a stress-free environment are essentials. If a fur farmer doesn't do that, he's shortly out of business. That is why animals raised for their fur are inherently the best cared for farm animals.[23]

Fur trapping

In addition to breeding and raising mink on farms, people obtain mink by trapping them in the wild. There are approximately 150,000 trappers in the United States. Annually, these trappers catch approximately 160,000 mink, which are not an endangered species.

In the United States one of the most common traps used is the steel-jaw leg-hold trap. The steel-jaw leg-hold trap is a restraining trap, meaning that it is made to catch animals but not kill them. When an animal steps in the trap, a spring-loaded steel jaw clamps on the animal's foot or leg. After trappers find a mink caught in the trap, they kill it for its pelt. According to the National Trappers Association, methods for killing mink include bludgeoning or shooting the animals.

Trappers must abide by state and local laws and regulations that determine what time of the year they may trap mink and how many mink they may trap during the season. Some local laws also require that their traps be checked once every twenty-four to thirty-six hours in order to prevent animals from being trapped and in pain for excessive periods of time. Penalties for violating trapping laws include revoking a hunter's trapping license or requiring that the hunter pay a fine.

Trapping concerns

Animal rights advocates and many animal welfare supporters believe that stricter laws and regulations are needed to reduce the stress and pain trapped mink endure. Specifically, they want the United States to enact a law that makes the steel-jaw leg-hold trap illegal. These advocates believe that this trap causes mink and other animals caught in it excessive pain.

According to animal behaviorist Desmond Morris, the shock to animals trapped in steel-jaw leg-hold traps is "difficult for us to conceive, because it is a shock of total lack of understanding of what has happened to them. They are held, they cannot escape, their response very often is to bite at the metal with their teeth, break their teeth in the process and sometimes even chew through the leg that is being held in the trap."[24]

Another criticism of the steel-jaw leg-hold trap and all other traps is that because they are not made to catch a specific animal, any animal that walks into a trap can get caught. Annually, according to the Humane Society (HSUS), millions of nontarget animals get caught in traps, and those caught in the steel-jaw leg-hold traps suffer from severe wounds and painful deaths as a result. The National Trappers Association argues that the HSUS number is exaggerated and that each year only about 120,000 nontarget animals are captured in the United States.

Due to the campaigns against the steel-jaw leg-hold trap, there have been some changes in trapping methods. As an example, some trappers now use a new padded leg-hold trap. In this trap thin strips of rubber are fastened on the jaws to reduce limb injuries. Another result of the campaigns is that eight states and approximately eighty countries have banned the use of the steel-jaw leg-hold trap.

Antifur campaigns

Animal rights and many animal welfare organizations want more than a ban of the steel-jaw leg-hold trap. They want to abolish the fur industry. Because these activists believe that killing animals to make a luxury item, such as a fur coat, is unethical, they have organized antifur campaigns. Due to widespread publicity, their campaigns have gained many supporters in the past three decades.

Antifur campaigns often involve celebrities to gain people's attention and support. In one of the most well-known

campaigns, celebrities posed naked in PETA's "I'd Rather Go Naked than Wear Fur" ads in magazines. Celebrities such as Pamela Anderson and Kim Basinger have participated in the ads.

PETA members protest the wearing of fur. They believe killing animals for their fur is unethical.

Despite the efforts of antifur campaigners, recent trends indicate that fur may be gaining popularity. According to the USDA, fur farms produced and sold 2.6 million fur pelts in 2002 compared to 2.56 million in 2001. Additionally, more fashion designers are including furs in their fashion shows. "In spite of the events of 9/11, a weak economy and the warmest winter on record, fur sales continued at a strong pace proving that it is an essential element in a woman's wardrobe," explains Keith Kaplan, executive director of the Fur Information Council of America. "In 1985, only 42 fashion designers were using fur in their ready-to-wear collections. Today, there are more than 300 renowned fashion designers showing fur fashions, coats and fur-trimmed merchandise."[25]

Animals and cosmetics

In addition to protesting the fur industry, animal activists focus on abolishing the use of animals in the cosmetics industry. Cosmetics are often tested on animals to determine the potential toxicity, or harmful effects, of the products. Makeup, shampoos, and hair spray are among the products tested on animals to ensure that they are safe for humans. Government agencies such as the Food and Drug Administration (FDA) and the Consumer Product Safety Division must approve the safety of cosmetics before companies can sell their products to the public.

The New Jersey Association for Biomedical Research estimates that about fifty thousand animals per year are used for testing personal care products. The tests include eye irritancy tests, skin irritancy tests, and ingestion tests.

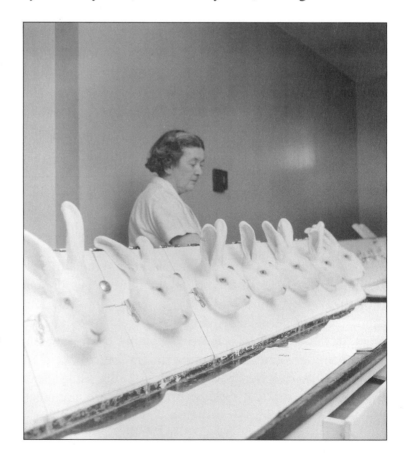

Restrained rabbits are prepared to undergo testing. Animal rights groups oppose using animals to determine the safety of beauty products.

Animals that undergo product testing may experience pain or death, depending on the type of test conducted and the type of product being tested. For three decades animal rights advocates have conducted publicity campaigns specifically focused on eliminating the Draize test and the LD50 test, two commonly known personal care product tests. Their efforts have resulted in several companies developing and using alternative tests that result in fewer animals dying.

Draize and LD50

The Draize test, a test for eye irritancy, was developed in the 1940s. It typically uses six or more albino rabbits because they have large, unpigmented eyes in which inflammation and irritation are relatively easy to observe. The rabbits are immobilized by placing them in holding devices from which their heads protrude. Then the products being tested, such as shampoo, are dropped into the rabbits' eyes. Their eyelids are held open by metal clips so that they cannot blink the substance out of their eyes. The product is placed into the rabbits' eyes several times to determine its harmful effects, if any. In some cases the rabbits' eyes are anesthetized before the test.

LD50, Lethal Dose 50 Percent, has been used since the 1920s. This test determines the lethal dose of the product if ingested. In the past, the lethal dosage was always determined by administering the product to one hundred animals in increasing doses until 50 percent of the animals died. The standard LD50 technique, still used by some companies today, requires the use of from sixty to two hundred animals, usually mice.

Historically, the LD50 and Draize tests have proven to be accurate tests. Because of the LD50 and Draize tests' reliability, in the past many companies were not willing to develop or use nonanimal testing methods out of fear that the tests would be inaccurate and that regulatory agencies such as the FDA would not accept them as proof of a product's safety. However, protests against companies who test their products on animals have led to changes in testing methods.

Animal testing changes

In the 1970s, due to animal welfare and rights organizations' efforts, people became more aware of the tests conducted on animals. For example, in 1978 animal rights activist Henry Spira initiated efforts to force Revlon, a major cosmetics company, to fund research into finding an alternative nonanimal test to replace the Draize test. His efforts included gaining the support of animal welfare and animal rights organizations by sending them pictures of rabbits' eyes harmed by the Draize test. These organizations sent letters to their members to convince them to campaign against Revlon until the company funded the alternative research. Additionally, Spira took out a full-page advertisement in the *New York Times*, which posed the incendiary question, "How many rabbits has Revlon blinded for beauty's sake?"

After learning about the details of the Draize test, many people began sending protest letters to Revlon and boycotting its products because they felt it was morally wrong to harm animals in order to make products, like mascara, that serve only to enhance a person's beauty. In 1981 Spira and his supporters' efforts resulted in Revlon allocating $750,000 to research for an alternative to the Draize test.

Today several cosmetic companies, including Revlon, do not use the Draize test and instead use tests that were developed due to the research for alternatives. For example, the MatTek EpiOcular test is designed to model the human corneal epithelium, the covering of the cornea, by using in vitro tissue, human tissue that is in a test tube. The products are tested on this model to determine their effects on the eyes.

In addition to alternatives for the Draize test, the LD50 test has been altered, resulting in less use of and fewer deaths of animals. One new method to test the lethal ingestion dose of products, called the up and down procedure (UDP), uses significantly fewer animals than the LD50 test. An animal is given the product and, based on its reaction, the product dosage is adjusted up or down and given to another animal. The UDP uses only eight animals per test on average. A computer is used to calculate an estimated lethal dose based on the animals' reactions.

Alternative acceptance

Despite the alternatives now available to the Draize test, LD50 test, and other product tests, the United States still uses thousands of animals a year in personal product tests. One of the reasons that some U.S. companies continue to test products on animals is that the companies must prove to U.S. regulatory agencies such as the FDA that their products are safe. Most regulatory agencies do not require animal testing but encourage it because they believe it

Activists protest Procter & Gamble's use of the Draize test on rabbits. Protests have led to more humane testing methods.

gives accurate results. According to the Humane Society of the United States (HSUS),

> In the United States, few laws actually mandate specific types of animal testing, but some regulations (which implement laws) do specify animal testing. The most common situation, however, is that animal testing is encouraged by a regulatory environment that has historically relied on such testing, thereby developing expectations and biases among regulators as well as corporate toxicologists.[26]

To encourage companies to use alternatives to animal testing, the U.S. government passed the Interagency Coordinating Committee on the Validation of Alternative Methods (ICCVAM) Authorization Act in 2000. This act officially formed the ICCVAM. The ICCVAM includes members from agencies such as the FDA and Consumer Product Safety Commission who decide whether or not to approve alternatives to using animals for product testing. If an alternative test receives approval, companies are more likely to use it because they are assured that government regulatory agencies will accept the alternative test's results as proof of the safety of a company's product.

With the ICCVAM's approvals of alternative tests, more U.S. companies are producing "cruelty-free" products, products that have not been tested on animals. In the past decade, approximately 550 U.S. companies, such as Avon and Gillette, signed a pledge that they will not conduct animal testing. As animal rights organizations remain dedicated to persuading consumers through ads, Web sites, and protests that using animals for beauty and fashion is immoral, it is likely that animal use in the cosmetics and fur industries will continue to decrease.

5

Animals in Entertainment

FROM ACTING IN movies to performing at circuses, animals often entertain people. Animal rights and animal welfare organizations have focused on improving the lives of animals that are in the public eye. They have initiated campaigns for humane treatment of performing animals. Many of these campaigns have targeted the television and film industry because this industry employs thousands of animals.

Since the early 1950s animals had starring roles in films and television. In 1951 a chimpanzee played a key role in the movie *Bedtime for Bonzo,* and during the next decade a Palomino horse played the main character of the television show *Mr. Ed.* In 1994 Marcel the monkey was a supporting character in the television comedy *Friends.* Four years later a pig played the leading role of the film *Babe.*

Animal agencies

Producers of movies and television typically hire animal actors from animal agencies. The Hollywood Animals' Animal Actors Agency has obtained, trained, and provided animal actors for films and television for over thirty years. Animal agencies like this find animals for movies and television from a variety of sources. Agencies often find domestic animals, such as dogs and cats, from listings by pet owners.

Agencies acquire wild animals, such as tigers and elephants, from importers or breeders. Before these animals are available to perform, an animal trainer teaches them to follow commands that the animals might need to know on a production set.

American Humane Association oversight

When animals first started acting for television and film, there was little oversight of the animals' treatment. Often the animals were subjected to risky stunts. During the 1939

TV's Mr. Ed (left) and canine star Big Red pose with their American Humane Association (AHA) awards in 1963. The AHA oversees the treatment of animal actors.

production of the film *Jesse James*, a horse and its rider jumped off a cliff. The horse died in the fall while the rider survived. When the public learned about this incident, it called for stricter animal supervision.

After the production of *Jesse James*, the American Humane Association (AHA), whose mission is to promote the welfare of both animals and children, opened an office in Los Angeles, California. Its Hollywood office is dedicated to protecting animal actors. In 1980, when the AHA was entrusted with the sole authority to protect animals in film and television, it developed regulations for their treatment. The regulations specify that no animal may be killed or harmed during a show's production; that no animal may be treated inhumanely to force a performance, such as by using trip wires to cause a horse to fall; and that all fishing and hunting scenes are simulated.

AHA gets involved with film projects before they are produced. "AHA works closely with trainers and producers to analyze and plan all the animal action during pre-production," states the AHA Web site. "We ensure that stunts, safety measures, camera angles, special effects, and even lighting, make-up and costumes for animal actors receive the same planning and consideration as for human stars."[27]

During production, AHA representatives visit production sites to confirm that the animals are treated well. If standards are followed, the film receives the AHA seal of approval, which is listed in the movie's credits. In a typical year the AHA reviews 850 film and television productions.

Animal actor concerns

Despite the AHA oversight, many people are concerned that animal abuse still occurs on film sets. For example, Clyde, the orangutan who starred with Clint Eastwood in the 1982 movie, *Every Which Way You Can*, was allegedly beaten during the movie's filming. Clyde died and an autopsy revealed that he had died of a cerebral hemorrhage, which some say may have been caused by repeated blows to the head.

PETA claims that Clyde's alleged abuse is not a one-time incident. Ingrid Newkirk, cofounder of PETA, writes:

> Whistle-blowers from films and filmed advertisements have complained of animal "actors" collapsing from the heat of the bright arc lights, being deprived of food, being prodded and goaded, and being scared by the clapboards or gunfire. Abuse can be as subtle as forcing cats to stay awake for hours so as to be able to get them to fall asleep "on cue," or the use of a "tie-down," an invisible filament wrapped around an animal's waist and attached to an unseen anchor.[28]

Newkirk claims that abuse such as this occurs despite the fact that AHA regulations prohibit it.

To ensure that they cannot possibly violate AHA regulations, many film and television producers have turned to using alternatives for live animals. Animatronics, robots that look like animals, and computer simulation are among the alternatives. In the Robert Redford film *A River Runs Through It*, where many scenes involved fishing, mechanical salmon were used rather than live fish.

Animal activists have also voiced concerns about what happens to animals after their film career is over. In the past, if no other home could be found, animal actors were euthanized. In response, in 1984 Pat Derby and partner Ed Stewart founded the Performing Animal Welfare Society (PAWS), an organization dedicated to finding homes for retired performing animals. Today, with help and sponsorship from its over thirty thousand members, PAWS has created three sanctuaries for captive wildlife, giving performing animals a home.

Live acts

In addition to appearing in movies and television, animals perform in live shows. Each year millions of adults and children watch animals perform in circuses, marine shows, and private events. The majority of animals used in these shows are exotic animals such as tigers, lions, elephants, dolphins, and bears, normally found in the wild.

Shows obtain exotic animals by breeding them, hiring them from animal agencies, or purchasing them from importers, people who capture animals in the wild and then bring them to the United States. After the animals are obtained, they are paired with a trainer who oversees their care and performance.

Many trainers develop close relationships with the animals and treat their animals with respect. Brian J. McMillan, the owner and founder of Hollywood Animals Exotic

Trained killer whales perform at an amusement park. Animal rights activists say living in captivity stresses the animals.

Animals Training School, emphasizes caring when he trains people to become animal trainers. He teaches his students that they are responsible for understanding and fulfilling their animals' needs. Ringling Bros. and Barnum & Bailey circus teaches the same to its animal trainers. On its Web site, Ringling Bros. and Barnum & Bailey states that its animal trainers "devote their lives to working with and caring for animals 24 hours a day, 365 days a year. The training and handling of all of our animals are based on constant contact, daily routines, and nurturing. This interaction builds a rapport between animals and handlers based on trust, respect and affection."[29]

Daily life

To ensure that performing animals' basic needs are met, the Animal Welfare Act (AWA) sets standards for the care of animals. For example, it stipulates that show animals' housing must be safe and provide protection from extreme temperatures. AWA housing requirements specify that tanks for marine mammals such as dolphins must be at least twenty-four feet wide and six feet deep. The AWA does not give specific space requirements for exotic animals, such as tigers, that are in traveling shows, but does cite that the animals must have adequate room. This requirement is satisfied if the animal is in a cage with enough space for it to walk or run or if the animal is periodically released from its cage to exercise in a ring.

Show animals typically receive a nutritious diet and good medical care. The AWA requires that animals receive adequate nutrition and necessary veterinary treatment. The USDA sends inspectors to the shows to ensure that the animals are being treated in accordance with the AWA.

Although adhering to the AWA is costly and takes much effort, show owners are willing to abide by it in part because exotic animals attract millions of spectators each year. These spectators are willing to pay high admission prices to see the animal exhibits.

Promoting animal education

Proponents of live animal shows claim that some of the money generated by these shows goes toward promoting animal welfare. The Alliance of Marine Mammals, a worldwide association of forty marine parks, aquariums, zoos, scientific research facilities, and professional organizations whose members must be dedicated to the conservation of marine animals and their environment, says that live shows fund research that benefits these animals. Additionally, it reports that over 36 million adults and children visit its member facilities each year and learn about animals through presentations, exhibits, and live shows.

The Alliance of Marine Mammals, Parks and Aquariums also claims that organizations that produce live acts, such as marine shows, help protect animal species through rescue programs and by conducting and funding scientific research. For example, it reports that in five years, from 1993 to 1998, its members rescued, rehabilitated, and released sixteen hundred stranded animals. These wild marine mammals, found sick and dying on beaches, were rescued through voluntary networks of members dedicated to saving mammals who are stranded. They were able to provide the stranded mammals with needed care because of the alliance members' research and medical studies of mammals. The Alliance asks,

> Without the marine life parks, aquariums, and zoos that participate in voluntary stranding networks, who would care for stranded seals, sea otters, manatees, and seals that find themselves sick or injured on our shores? Who would continue the advances that have led to the successful rehabilitation and release of a greater number of dolphins and whales in recent years—animals that are generally very sick or injured when found?[30]

Captive animal concerns

Despite education and preservation achievements of the circuses, marine exhibits, and private animal shows, there are several concerns about capturing wild animals and placing them in captivity. Animal rights activists claim that

Marine park scientists rescue a stranded whale. Most parks emphasize rescue and conservation of animals.

transporting animals from their native homes in the wild to shows or parks thousands of miles away causes stress-related health problems. For example, in July 2003 twenty-eight dolphins were flown 12,800 miles from the Solomon Islands in the South Pacific Ocean to their new home in Cancún, Mexico. The Mexico-based Parque Nizuc, a tourist attraction where people can swim with the dolphins, had purchased the dolphins and flown them across the ocean to the park. Within one week, one of the dolphins died. An autopsy by park veterinarians discovered the dolphin had suffered from various stomach ulcers due to stress-related complications.

Animal rights advocates also believe that animals live a more stressful life in captivity than they would in the wild.

One reason cited is that captive animals cannot roam freely, which is important for their emotional health. Studies have shown that confined animals show signs of stress such as pacing and repetitive behavior. Wild tigers roam for miles in the wild, but tigers in circuses live in cages or enclosed areas. Free dolphins normally swim forty to one hundred miles daily, but dolphins in marine shows live in tanks where the required tank size is 24 by 24 by 6 feet.

Another concern of animal rights supporters is that despite the Animal Welfare Act (AWA), show animals are subject to abuse. For example, in 2003 the USDA was provided with video footage of an elephant being beaten by a Clyde Beatty–Cole Bros. Circus employee. A resident of Charleston, South Carolina, had caught the beating on tape while Beatty-Cole was performing in that city. The employee was forcefully striking an elephant on her leg and head with a broom. The USDA fined the circus $2,750 for improper handling of an elephant.

Public response

Critics of live animal acts encourage people to attend nonanimal alternatives. In fact, attendance at nonanimal circuses like the Cirque du Soleil has risen in recent years. The Cirque du Soleil performs all around the world, using people, as opposed to animals, in its main acts. Responding to animal rights efforts to deter people from attending circuses with animals, a Ringling Bros. and Barnum & Bailey representative states, "We believe in the healthy interaction of animals and humans, not the 'separatism' as espoused by the cultists which would deny our children the opportunity to experience not only the beauty of animals firsthand, but to observe harmony that can exist when humans and animals work and play together."[31]

The public has also supported animal rights and animal welfare campaigns to free captive animals. In 1993 kids and adults saw *Free Willy*, a movie about a boy saving a captive whale. People discovered that Keiko, the orca who played Willy in the movie, resided in a tank in a Mexico City amusement park. He had a compromised immune system,

Keiko the killer whale is released into the wild. Activists' efforts helped free the orca from captivity.

was severely underweight, and suffered from muscle atrophy (weak muscles). Upon learning this, people and animal organizations banded together to form the Free Willy/Free Keiko foundation.

Due to this foundation and public support, Keiko was eventually moved to a rehabilitation facility to restore the orca's health. Keiko was taught to hunt and in 1998 was released in Icelandic waters.

Dog and horse racing

Dog and horse races are another form of animal entertainment for humans. People attend greyhound and horse racetracks to bet on how well specific horses and dogs will perform in the races. In 1998 people wagered $2.2 billion on U.S. greyhound racing and in 2002 people bet over $15 billion on U.S. horse racing.

Greyhound owners obtain the dogs by either breeding or buying them from breeders. The owners typically lease their greyhounds to a kennel that is contracted by a racing track. The kennel is responsible for caring for the greyhounds and, when the dogs begin to race, pays the owner usually 35 percent of the winnings the greyhounds earn during their racing career. When the greyhounds are fifteen to eighteen months old, they are sent from the kennels to live at their tracks. At the track, the greyhounds get to know their trainers, who teach the dogs to run around the track while following a lure. After training, the greyhounds typically race two times a week and exercise in between races.

Race horse owners also either purchase their horses from breeders or breed their own. Often the owner boards his horse on a farm where a trainer familiarizes the horse with running on racetracks, building the horse's speed and endurance. The horse's trainer selects the races in which the horse will compete, and jockeys ride the horses during the races. The owner, trainer, and jockey all receive a part of the horse's racing winnings.

As valuable assets, these racehorses receive the best of care. Critics, however, say the animals' moneymaking value eclipses their welfare.

Throughout their lives, racing dogs and horses typically receive good nutrition, housing, and veterinary care. The trainers spend much time with the dogs and horses, overseeing their feeding, exercise, veterinary care, and training. Ensuring that the dogs and horses remain healthy is in both the trainers' and owners' best interest. According to the Greyhound Racing Association of America, the greyhound "pups—from birth throughout their training—receive abundant attention from their owners, trainers and handlers, including a lot of play. An unhappy dog will not learn as quickly or as well, nor will he run as well."[32]

Racing concerns and responses

Despite the fact that many owners and trainers provide good care for their animals, critics of horse and dog racing claim that because money is involved in the races, the animals' best interests are not always considered. For example, animal rights activists charge that horse owners take actions that will give their horses the best chance at winning even at the expense of the animal's health. Giving horses drugs to mask pain is an example of such an action, according to racing critics. If a horse is injured and given these drugs, the horse will run just as hard as if it were not injured. When horses race with injuries, they are at risk of causing greater injury to themselves.

An article in the *Washington Post* reported that all horses that raced at the 2003 Kentucky Derby were given a shot of Lasix, a legal drug that controls bleeding in the lungs and masks pain. Additionally, the article claimed that most horses were probably given phenylbutazone, a legal anti-inflammatory drug that also masks pain.

Horse professionals contend that legal drugs like Lasix are not used to enhance performance but to treat health problems. They state the veterinarians must give approval for the horses to receive these drugs. According to the U.S. Trotting Association, a horse that is going to race must show signs that it is suffering from bleeding in the lungs before a veterinarian will treat the horse with Lasix.

A criticism of dog racing is that the greyhounds' only purpose is to produce profit for its owners and trainers. The HSUS Web site reports that "Unfortunately, the industry kills greyhounds at various stages in the dogs' lives because they appear to lack racing potential or are injured. Many dogs, when they are no longer profitable, are adopted into good homes through rescue groups, but thousands are not."[33] According to the HSUS, in the year 2000 approximately 11,400 former greyhound racers were euthanized.

To reduce the number of greyhounds euthanized each year, both animal welfare groups and greyhound professional racing organizations have formed several greyhound adoption agencies in the past decade. These organizations persuade the public to adopt these animals as pets. Racetracks contribute more than $1 million annually to local adoption greyhound efforts. As a result, approximately eighteen thousand greyhounds that have retired from racing are adopted each year.

The adoption of greyhounds and similar efforts for animals in other entertainment industries indicate the growing level of public concern for these animals. If the public stays focused on the lives of performing animals, it is likely that the animals will continue to receive better treatment and oversight.

6

Preserving Wild Animals

MOST AMERICANS AGREE that humans must protect animal species from becoming endangered or extinct. However, there is disagreement over how this should be accomplished. Many believe that the best ways to preserve animal species are to breed and house animals in protected environments like zoos and to hunt wild animals to control rampant populations. Animal rights advocates argue that in order to preserve animal species, humans must not interfere with animals' lives or their natural habitats. Because of this disagreement, zoos and hunting as a way to protect animals are the source of much debate.

Until recently the only purpose of a zoo was to exhibit captive animals, not protect them. The concept of exhibiting animals dates back to at least 1500 B.C. During this time Queen Hatshepsut of Egypt demonstrated her power and wealth by collecting animals from the wild and displaying them. By the seventeenth century private zoos had become common among the rich in Europe. After the discovery of the New World, explorers returned to Europe with exotic species obtained for aristocrats' private menageries.

The idea of a public zoo, where the general public could visit displays of animals, became popular throughout the United States and Europe in the nineteenth century. By the end of the twentieth century public zoos were established around the world and had millions of visitors annually. According to the Humane Society of the United States, in the United States alone there are over 2,000 animal exhibitors. Of these, 213 belong to the American Zoo and Aquarium Association (AZA), the largest professional association of zoos. The AZA reports that its zoos and aquarium members drew over 134 million visitors in the year 2000.

Zoo guidelines

All American zoos must abide by the federal Animal Welfare Act (AWA). This law requires that zoos provide the basic requirements such as safe housing, nutrition, and veterinary care to their animals. U.S. Department of Agriculture (USDA) inspectors visit zoos to ensure that these standards are met and that all animals receive good care.

In addition to following the guidelines of the AWA, zoos that belong to professional organizations such as the AZA

A young zoo patron views elephants in their enclosure. Whether zoos benefit or harm animals is an ongoing debate.

must abide by these organizations' regulations in order to receive the organization's accreditation. These regulations often go beyond meeting animals' basic needs. AZA guidelines include regulations that are meant to enrich the animals' lives. For example, the AZA requires that zoos provide elephants a water source, such as a waterfall, so that the elephants are able to bathe themselves. Because of the AZA's regulations and focus on enriching animals' lives, zoos have developed more natural exhibits. These exhibits often include more room for animals to roam and environments replicated after animals' natural habitats.

Zoo education

By the latter half of the 1900s many zoo directors believed that in addition to displaying animals for people to enjoy, zoos should educate people about these species. Directors of the zoos that are members of the AZA are re-

Many zoos provide programs for patrons to learn about, not just view, animals. Advocates and critics disagree on the value of such programs.

quired to include public education in their zoo's written mission. These directors believe that the more people learn about the animals they view at zoos, the more likely they will develop a lifelong interest in the well-being and conservation of these animals. Zoo directors hope that this interest will encourage people to support conservation initiatives such as campaigns to help save endangered species. According to Lewis Greene, executive director of the Virginia Zoo in Norfolk, Virginia, "I look at all the animals we have in the zoo as ambassadors to their species. We're giving them a chance to be seen and talked about. If we get people to care about them, they may be moved to do something for them."[34]

To educate the public, zoos have displays throughout, such as signs by an animal's exhibit describing the animal and its natural habitat, and offer presentations to the public by zookeepers who describe the habits of the animals. Additionally, zoos offer special student and teacher programs. For instance, over 9 million students a year attend onsite education programs at AZA zoos and aquariums, and 3.5 million of these students attend free of charge. Additionally, eighty-five thousand teachers a year attend AZA training workshops and obtain teaching materials about animals and their habitats. Through these programs people learn more about the threats animals face and what they can do to help protect animals.

Zoo supporters say efforts to involve the public are working. They point to the growing number of people who pay to become members of zoos and donate to zoo efforts. The AZA reports that over 2 million households in America are zoo or aquarium members and have provided over $96 million to fund zoo-supported research, such as studies to track patterns of animal disease in order to prevent future deaths, and animal protection initiatives. Additionally, in the year 2000 over fifty-eight thousand zoo volunteers gave more than 5 million hours of their time to AZA facilities.

Despite zoos' efforts, critics claim that zoos are not achieving their education goal. In 1991 Dale Marcellini, a curator of reptiles at the National Zoo in Washington, D.C., decided to study the habits of zoo visitors. He and his colleagues found that when visitors were at exhibits, they spent little time actually viewing and reading about the animals. Marcellini found that visitors spent less than eight seconds per snake and only one minute with the lions. Critics of zoos use studies like Marcellini's to argue that zoos' education efforts do not result in people understanding or caring more about animals.

Zoo preservation

Zoo professionals claim that zoos not only educate the public but also shield weak and old animals from vicious predators, extreme temperatures, and other ravages of nature. They also claim that they protect animal species from extinction. In their written mission, AZA zoos must include the goal to preserve animal species. To achieve this goal, AZA zoos participate in the Species Survival Plan (SSP), an AZA program with the mission of preserving selected species by means such as reintroducing captive-bred wildlife into restored or secure habitats and by organizing breeding programs to prevent the species' extinction. Most species are chosen to be in the SSP because they are endangered or threatened in the wild. In June 2003, 161 species were covered by the SSP.

Several AZA zoos participate in SSP projects. In 2003 the Virginia Zoo in Norfolk chose to send Ed, an eighteen-month-old bongo (a rare species of antelope) to the African country Kenya in an effort to repopulate that region with bongos. Bongos used to be plentiful in Africa, but over the years their numbers were depleted due to poaching and human encroachment on their land.

Ed, three other male bongos, and eighteen female bongos from zoos across the United States will live in a one-hundred-acre preserve in Kenya. Virginia Zoo executive director Greene believes this effort is an example of zoos taking an active role in preserving animal species throughout the world. "People in the past have seen zoos as consumers of wildlife," Greene explains. "Many zoos are now

working on giving something back, working to help the species in the wild."[35]

It is uncertain whether zoos provide animals like this lion the room they need to roam.

Zoo concerns

There is a concern that even with the AWA regulations and the AZA guidelines, captive animals' lives are full of boredom and stress. For example, critics point out that since only 10 percent of zoos are members of the AZA, the remaining 90 percent of zoos, unless they are members of another zoo organization, do not need to abide by AZA regulations that include requirements to help alleviate animals' boredom. Instead, these zoos are only required to provide the most basic care.

Animal rights advocates also claim that animals in zoos, including AZA zoos, experience stress because they do not have enough space to roam. They point to an Oxford University study by British biologist Georgia Mason that was published in *Nature*, a scientific journal, in October 2003. In her study of forty-two zoos and thirty-five species, Mason found that captive polar bears, lions, tigers, cheetahs, and other large predators that roam hundreds of miles in the wild, exhibited many symptoms of stress, such as pacing back and forth, nodding repetitively, and swaying the body repetitively. "Zoos need to think much more about giving these animals features of a large range—e.g., bigger enclosures, longer boundaries for patrolling, views that offer variety, more dens and sleeping places, and simply more day-to-day variety,"[36] Mason wrote.

Zookeepers address these concerns by trying to find ways to alleviate animals' boredom and provide greater space. For example, Jonathan Gilmour, zookeeper of Franklin Zoo in Boston works to keep zoo animals' lives interesting by using methods such as changing feeding stations around in the exhibits, introducing new kinds of foods, or hiding food so the animals must find it. Additionally, he tries to find ways to break up animals' routines by placing a new item or scent into their exhibits. Gilmour explains, "You'd be surprised how much mileage you can get out of a daily newspaper. Some of the animals can shred that for hours. Old pizza boxes are a favorite, too."[37]

Other zoo professionals such as Andy Baker, senior vice president for animal programs at the Philadelphia Zoo, are actively addressing space concerns. The Philadelphia Zoo has two female polar bears that live in a 20,000-square-foot enclosure with a 300,000-gallon pool. Zookeepers believe they are content because they rarely pace or exhibit signs of stress. Additionally, the Philadelphia Zoo, according to Baker, is providing more space to lions and tigers by setting up their exhibits so that they can roam into each other's area. Increasingly, other zoos are following the Franklin and Philadelphia Zoos' examples.

Hunting

Just as the role of zoos in animal preservation is debated, so too is the role of hunting. In 2001, 13 million Americans hunted a wide range of animals including deer, duck, and quail. Many of these Americans claim that hunting helps preserve animal species by controlling populations. If left to nature, hunters believe that wild animals continue to reproduce until there are so many animals that they cannot find enough food. Those that do not die of starvation are weakened by disease. Killing animals leaves the rest of the herd enough food to survive and keeps the next generation of animals healthy, according to hunters. In Maryland hunters harvested 94,114 white-tailed deer during 2003, and according to Department of Natural Resources (DNR) Wildlife and Heritage Service director Paul A. Peditto, without these hunters the deer population would be out of control. "The objective of Maryland's Comprehensive Deer Management Plan is to maintain healthy deer populations as a valuable component of our state's ecosystem,"[38] Peditto stated, claiming that without hunting, many of the deer would have faced the slow process of starvation.

To ensure that animal species thrive and are not depleted, hunters must abide by the federal and state hunting programs of the U.S. Fish and Wildlife Service (FWS). This government agency's mission includes protecting wildlife and nature. The FWS sets seasons for hunting migratory birds and other animals. It also limits the number of birds and animals that may be hunted annually and prohibits the hunting of endangered species. Hunters are also prohibited from harming the habitats of endangered animals.

Hunting and preservation

In the United States every state requires that hunters obtain licenses to hunt. Hunters must pay a fee to obtain the license. According to the National Rifle Association (NRA), in 2000 the 15.1 million hunters contributed over $580 million to state fish and wildlife agencies to receive their licenses. Hunting supporters point out that the money generated by hunting goes toward conservation and helping animal species survive. Since 1923 sales of state hunting licenses, tags, and permits have provided more

A hunter poses with his trophy. Some claim hunting helps preserve species and promote conservation.

than $9.1 billion toward programs such as wildlife management, wildlife habitat protection, acquisition of land for wildlife, and conservation law enforcement.

Saving sheep

Hunters point to the fact that money made from hunting has also helped protect animals in poorer countries. The Marco Polo sheep, a rare breed with helix-shaped horns that can exceed six feet in length, was once abundant in central Asian countries. By the 1970s the Marco Polo sheep population in Tajikistan had been significantly reduced. Due to the poverty in Tajikistan, residents killed the sheep for food and also to stop the sheep from eating their crops.

The Marco Polo sheep have become plentiful again in Tajikistan. Hunters claim this is because Tajikistan has opened the country to limited hunting of Marco Polo sheep and uses the money it receives from the hunters to conserve the country's animals, their habitats, and to assist the country's people.

Hunters from other countries are willing to pay much money for the privilege to hunt Tajikistan's Marco Polo sheep because it is illegal to hunt the endangered sheep in most countries, making them rare hunting trophies. Hunters claim that the money they spend in Tajikistan, which goes to the locals, stops them from poaching the sheep, and that the number of Marco Polo sheep hunted is much less than the number of sheep that are illegally

Hunters covet the horns of the Marco Polo sheep. Controlled hunting of the sheep has helped increase its numbers in some areas.

poached. "The [payoffs from hunters] to Tajiks has successfully ended poaching and subsistence hunting, and mitigates losses incurred by poor farmers and shepherds," writes Peter Spellmeyer, a member of the Foundation for North American Wild Sheep, who visited Tajikistan in 2003. "There is now a greater incentive to maintain a population of large and healthy sheep and ibex than to kill and eat them, and the sustainable removal of select animals represents the essential trade-off."[39]

Hunting concerns

Critics also disagree that hunting is needed in order to control animals' population. Animal welfare groups such as HSUS claim that hunting actually contributes to the growth of deer herds. "Heavily hunted states like Pennsylvania and Ohio, for instance, are among those experiencing higher deer densities than perhaps ever before," states the HSUS Web site. "When an area's deer population is reduced by hunting, the remaining animals respond by having more young, which survive because the competition for food and habitat is reduced."[40]

Due to concerns like these, hunting critics have used both legal and illegal methods to campaign against hunting. Their methods have ranged from picketing at hunting sites to sabotaging hunts by going in the woods and making loud noises to scare off the animals during hunting season. Despite the fact that American hunters have decreased from 21 million in 1980 to 13 million in 2002, animal rights activists are not satisfied. Ultimately, they believe that hunting and other interference by humans in animals' lives must stop in order to preserve animal species and their rights. However, public sentiment continues to be more aligned with the animal welfare groups that do not oppose human interaction with animals but support protecting and helping animals through means such as enriching zoo animals' lives.

Notes

Introduction

1. Quoted in Ellin Beltz, "1987 HerPET-POURRI," May 1987. www.ebeltz.net/column/1987colu.html.

2. Carl Cohen and Tom Regan, *The Animal Rights Debate.* Oxford, England: Rowman & Littlefield, 2001, p. 127.

3. National Association of Biology Teachers, "The Use of Animals in Biology Education," www.nabt.org/sub/position_statements/animals.asp.

Chapter 1: Do Animals Have Rights?

4. Gen. (1:28 New King James Version).

5. Quoted in Institute for Animal Rights Law, "Some Thoughts on the Rights of Animals," www.instituteforanimalrightslaw.org/articles_thoughts_on_animal_rights.htm.

6. Quoted in Peter Singer, "All Animals Are Equal," *PETA Guide to Animal Liberation*, p. 15.

7. Harold D. Guither, *Animal Rights: History and Scope of a Radical Social Movement.* Carbondale and Edwardsville: Southern Illinois University Press, 1998, p. 4.

8. Quoted in Rob Stein, "Research Shows Dogs Have In-born Talent to 'Read' Humans," *Virginian-Pilot*, August 22, 2003, p. AA6.

9. America's Charities, "Humane Society of the United States," www.charities.org/member/hsus.html.

10. Guither, *Animal Rights*, p. 13.

Chapter 2: Animals as Food

11. American Meat Institute, "The Ethical and Economic Reasons to Treat Animals Humanely," www.meatami.com/

content/presscenter/factsheets_Infokits/EthicalandEconomic
ReasonstoTreatAnimalsHumanely.pdf.

12. Carolyn Stull, Richard Warner, and Lowell Wilson, "Special Fed Veal," http://ars.sdstate.edu/animaliss/veal.html.

13. Cohen and Regan, *The Animal Rights Debate*, p. 137.

14. C.B. Tucker and D.M. Weary, "Tail Docking in Dairy Cattle," *Animal Welfare Information Center Bulletin*, Winter 2001–Spring 2002. www.nal.usda.gov/awic/newsletters/v11n3/11n3tuck.htm.

15. Quoted in National Pork Producers Council, "Voluntary Reforms in the Livestock Industry Have Changed the Way Animals Are Slaughtered," April 28, 2003. www.nppc.org/news/stories/2003/030429Welfare.html.

Chapter 3: Animals in Science

16. Quoted in Cohen and Regan, *The Animal Rights Debate*, p. 11.

17. Quoted in Judy Wieder, "Melissa Etheridge: The Advocate's Person of the Year," January 23, 1998. www.advocate.com/html/specials/melissa/698_99_melissa.asp.

18. Quoted in Humane Society of the United States, "Whistleblower Draws Scrutiny to Columbia University," October 2003. www.hsus.org/ace/20019.

19. Jeff Johnson, "'Animal Rights' Group Promotes Criminal 'Achievements,'" CNS News, January 22, 2002. www.cnsnews.com.

20. Quoted in Guither, *Animal Rights*, p. 80.

21. Quoted in Johns Hopkins Center for Alternatives to Animal Testing, "CAAT 20th Anniversary Symposium," September 2001. http://caat.jhsph.edu/programs/workshops/20th/schwetz.htm.

Chapter 4: Animals in Fashion and Cosmetics

22. Cohen and Regan, *The Animal Rights Debate*. p. 140.

23. Quoted in Delia Montgomery, "Fur Ethics," Fur Commission USA, November 2001. www.furcommission.com/resource/perspect999as.htm.

24. Quoted in Cohen and Regan, *The Animal Rights Debate.* p. 141.

25. Quoted in Fur Commission USA, "Fur Retail Sales Remain Strong in Unstable Economy," May 20, 2002. www.fur commission.com/news/newsF04w.htm.

26. Humane Society of the United States, "An Overview of Animal Testing Issues," http://files.hsus.org/web-files/PDF/ARIS_ An_Overview_Of_Animal_Testing_Issues.pdf.

Chapter 5: Animals in Entertainment

27. American Humane Association, "Protecting Animals in Film and Television," www.ahafilm.org/history.html.

28. Ingrid Newkirk, *You Can Save the Animals: 251 Simple Ways to Stop Animal Cruelty.* Rocklin, CA: Prima, 1999, p. 78.

29. Ringling Bros. and Barnum & Bailey, "Amazing Animals," www.ringling.com/animals.

30. Quoted in PBS, "A Whale of a Business," 1998. www. pbs.org/wgbh/pages/frontline/shows/whales.

31. Quoted in Guither, *Animal Rights*, p. 105.

32. Greyhound Racing Association of America, "Training at the Tracks," www.gra-america.org/training.html.

33. Humane Society of the United States, "Greyhound Racing Facts," www.hsus.org/ace/11798.

Chapter 6: Preserving Wild Animals

34. Quoted in Debbie Messina, "Bongo at Va. Zoo Being Sent to Africa," *Virginian-Pilot*, October 4, 2003, p. B4.

35. Quoted in Messina, "Bongo at Va. Zoo Being Sent to Africa," p. B4.

36. Quoted in Faye Flam, "Study: Animals Used to Roaming Fare Badly at Zoos," *Philadelphia Inquirer*, October 2, 2003. www.philly.com/mld/inquirer/news/front/6910373.htm.

37. Quoted in Jim Collins, "Animal Attractions," *U.S. Airways Attaché*, September 2003, p. 27.

38. Quoted in Gary Diamond, "Mid-Atlantic 2003 Outlook," *Mid-Atlantic Game & Fish*, October 5, 2003. www.mid atlanticgameandfish.com/at_aa100503a.

39. Quoted in Amanda Onion, "Hunt and Protect?" ABC News, May 7, 2002. http://abcnews.go.com/sections/scitech/DailyNews/sheephunting020507.html.

40. Humane Society of the United States, "Learn the Facts About Hunting," www.hsus.org/ace/12043?pg=3.

Glossary

animal welfare: The protection of the health and well-being of animals.

Animal Welfare Act: U.S. law passed in 1966 that sets the standards for the handling, housing, feeding, and caring of animals in laboratories, zoos, circuses, and pet stores.

cruelty-free products: Products that have not been tested on animals.

Draize test: Test that drops a product into rabbits' eyes to determine whether the product will cause irritation or harm in a person's eyes.

endangered species: Animals that are in danger of becoming extinct.

free-range farms: Farms where animals are given relative freedom to roam and forage.

fur farms: Farms where fur-bearing animals, such as mink, are raised for the use of their pelts.

intensive farming: Farming characterized by large-scale housing of animals and mechanization methods.

in vitro tests: Tests conducted outside of an animal or human body in an artificial environment.

Lethal Dose 50 Percent (LD50) test: Test that determines the lethal dose of a product when ingested. The product is repeatedly administered to a group of animals until 50 percent of the animals die.

sentient: The capacity to feel pain, to suffer, and to experience enjoyment.

threatened species: Animals that are likely to become endangered in the future.

utilitarianism: Basing decisions on what is the best total circumstance for both humans and animals.

vegan: A person who does not eat any form of meat, including beef, pork, fish, or chicken, or any animal products such as cheese, milk, and eggs.

vegetarian: A person who does not eat any form of meat including beef, pork, fish, and chicken.

vivisection: The cutting open of a live animal.

Organizations
to Contact

American Medical Association (AMA)

515 N. State St., Chicago, IL 60610
(800) 621-8335
www.ama-assn.org

The AMA's mission is to speak out on issues important to patients' and the nation's health. The AMA, which comprises physician delegates representing every state, opposes legislative limits placed on the use of animals in research and uses its public education program to advocate the appropriate and humane use of animals in research.

American Society for the Prevention of Cruelty to Animals (ASPCA)

424 E. 92nd St., New York, NY 10128
(212) 876-7700
www.aspca.org

Founded in 1866, the ASPCA is a humane organization dedicated to preventing cruelty to animals in the United States. It works toward this mission by providing national programming and leadership in humane education, public awareness of animal issues, animal shelter support, animal medical services, and animal placement.

American Zoo and Aquarium Association (AZA)

8403 Colesville Rd., Suite 710
Silver Springs, MD 20910-3314
(301) 562-0777
fax: (301) 562-0888
www.aza.org

The AZA, an American nonprofit organization founded in 1924, is made up of 213 accredited zoo and aquarium members. These members receive accreditation by adhering to AZA standards on animal collection, veterinary care, physical facilities, safety, security, finance, staff, governing authority, support organization, involvement in education, conservation, and research.

Animal Welfare Institute (AWI)

PO Box 3650, Washington, DC 20027
(703) 836-4300
fax: (703) 836-0400
www.awionline.org

Established in 1951, AWI is a nonprofit charitable organization that works to reduce the pain and fear inflicted on animals by humans. Its aims include the preservation of species threatened with extinction, banning use of the steel-jaw leghold trap, reforming treatment of farm animals, and reforming the handling of laboratory animals.

Fur Commission USA

PMB 506, 826 Orange Ave., Coronado, CA 92118-2698
(619) 575-0139
fax: (619) 575-5578
email: furfarmers@aol.com
www.furcommission.com

Fur Commission USA comprises 420 mink-farming families on 330 farms in 28 states. It sets standards of animal husbandry for its fur-farm members, educates the public about responsible fur farming, and about its beliefs as to the merits of fur.

Humane Society of the United States (HSUS)

2100 L St. NW, Washington, DC 20037
(202) 452-1100
www.hsus.org

Established in 1954, HSUS is an animal welfare organization that seeks to achieve a society where animals are respected for their intrinsic value, and where the human-animal bond is strong. HSUS is not opposed to what it considers legitimate uses of animals, such as certain animal research, but is opposed to animal use such as trapping animals for fur.

In Defense of Animals (IDA)

131 Camino Alto, Mill Valley, CA 94941
(415) 388-9641
fax: (415) 388-0388
email: ida@idausa.org
www.idausa.org

IDA, a nonprofit organization founded in 1983, is dedicated to ending the exploitation and abuse of animals. IDA works to achieve this by coordinating protests against what IDA considers animal abuses, conducting educational campaigns about animal rights, rescuing abused and abandoned animals, and pressuring laboratories to release animals.

National Rifle Association (NRA)

NRA Development Office, 11250 Waples Mill Rd.,
Fairfax, VA 22030
(703) 267-1130
www.nra.org

The NRA, the largest American organization of gun owners with over 4 million members, provides firearms education to people throughout the United States. A proponent of hunting, the NRA publishes monthly hunting magazines such as the *American Hunter* and provides updates on hunting information on its Web site.

People for the Ethical Treatment of Animals (PETA)

501 Front St., Norfolk, VA 23510
(757) 622-7382
www.peta.org

Established in 1980, PETA is an animal rights organization with over 750,000 members worldwide. PETA believes that animals are not for humans to eat, wear, experiment on, or use for entertainment. PETA educates policy makers and the public about what it considers animal abuse and runs various campaigns to end these abuses.

U.S. Department of Agriculture (USDA)

Washington, DC 20250
email: vic.powell@usda.gov
www.usda.gov

The goals of the USDA, a government organization founded in 1862, include ensuring that a safe, affordable, nutritious, and accessible food supply exists for the American people; caring for agricultural, forest, and range lands; supporting sound development of rural communities; providing economic opportunities for farm and rural residents; expanding global markets for agricultural and forest products and services; and working to reduce hunger in America and throughout the world.

U.S. Fish and Wildlife Service

Administration Office, Main Interior, 1849 C St. NW, Room 3238, Washington, DC 20240-0001
(202) 208-4717
fax: (202) 208-6965
www.fws.gov

The U.S. Fish and Wildlife Service, a federal agency under the Department of Interior, works to conserve, protect, and enhance fish, wildlife, plants, and their habitats for the continuing benefit of the American people. The organization's goals include saving endangered species, conserving migratory birds, preserving wildlife habitat, restoring fisheries, combating invasive species, and promoting international wildlife conservation.

For Further Reading

Books

Jennifer Hurley, ed., *Animal Rights,* San Diego: Greenhaven, 1999. Through articles written by different authors, this book presents a variety of opinions regarding animal rights issues. Among the issues addressed are medical research using animals, hunting, and whether animals are born with inherent rights.

Barbara Jones, *Animal Rights.* Austin, TX: Raintree Steck-Vaughn, 1999. This title explores different views and thoughts regarding animal rights and related issues.

Deidre Rochard, *Rights for Animals?* Danbury, CT: Franklin Watts, 1996. This book provides information on both sides of the animal rights debate. It explores issues such as animal use in science, clothing, and agriculture.

Anastasia Suen, *ASPCA: The American Society for Prevention of Cruelty to Animals.* New York: Powerkids, 2002. This title explores the ASPCA's history and its current animal welfare goals and campaigns.

Kelly Wand, ed., *The Animal Rights Movement.* San Diego: Greenhaven, 2002. This book contains excerpts from books and periodicals from the last three decades. The excerpts give different viewpoints of various animal rights issues. The excerpts cover topics such as the goals of animal welfare organizations such as ASPCA and animal rights organizations such as PETA.

Geraldine Woods, *Animal Experimentation and Testing.* Berkeley Heights, NJ: Enslow, 1999. This title explores the use of animals in medical experiments and whether it is both ethical and practical.

Internet Sources

Hattie Brown, "Educators, Animal Rights Advocates Debate Importance of Dissection," University of Maryland Philip Merrill College of Journalism, October 11, 2002. www.journalism.umd.edu/cns/wire/2002-editions/10-October-editions/021011-Friday/DissectionDebate_CNS_UMCP.html.

Free Willy Keiko Foundation, "Frequently Asked Questions About Keiko," www.keiko.com/faq.html.

Web Sites

Animal Land (www.animaland.org). Sponsored by the ASPCA, this Web site contains information about animal welfare issues and provides information on how to help improve the treatment of animals.

AZA's Campaign News (http://www.azasweb.com/default.aspx?tabindex=0&tabid=1). Sponsored by the American Zoo and Aquarium Association, this Web site includes suggestions for how adults and children can protect and save the world's animals and their environment.

Works Consulted

Books

Carl Cohen and Tom Regan, *The Animal Rights Debate.*
Oxford, England: Rowman & Littlefield, 2001. The authors
of this book are both philosophers with opposing views of
animal rights. Regan, who believes that animals have rights,
and Cohen, who believes that animals do not have rights,
discuss their beliefs.

C. Ray Greek and Jean Swingle Greek, *Sacred Cows and
Golden Geese: The Human Cost of Experiments on Animals.*
New York: Continuum International, 2000. The authors of
this book argue that the use of animals in experiments is
unnecessary and produces inaccurate results.

Harold D. Guither, *Animals Rights: History and Scope of a
Radical Social Movement.* Carbondale and Edwardsville:
Southern Illinois University Press, 1998. This book discusses animal rights and its related issues from an objective
viewpoint. Animal use in farming, clothing, science, hunting, and entertainment is among the book's topics.

Kathleen Marquardt with Herbert M. Levine and Mark La
Rochelle, *Animal Scam: The Beastly Abuse of Human
Rights.* Washington, DC: Regnery, 1993. This author is the
founder of the anti–animal rights group, Putting People
First. She opposes the goals of animal rights groups. In this
book the author discusses why animal use in areas such as
fur production and food production is necessary.

Ingrid Newkirk, *You Can Save the Animals: 251 Simple
Ways to Stop Animal Cruelty.* Rocklin, CA: Prima, 1999.
Newkirk, cofounder of PETA, writes about various animal
rights issues, from animal use in circuses and zoos to animal

use in testing. She provides arguments for why animal use is wrong and describes ways people can help protect animals from such use.

Periodicals and Pamphlets

Jim Collins, "Animal Attractions," *U.S. Airways Attaché*, September 2003.

Economist, "Monkey See, Monkey Do," October 18, 2003.

Debbie Messina, "Bongo at Va. Zoo Being Sent to Africa," *Virginian-Pilot*, October 4, 2003.

Richard C. Paddock and Richard Boudreaux, "On Solomon Islands, Dolphin Trade Sparks Protest," *Virginian-Pilot*, November 21, 2003.

Jeremy Rifkin, "A Change of Heart About Animals," *Virginian-Pilot*, September 7, 2003.

Peter Singer, "All Animals Are Equal," *PETA Guide to Animal Liberation.*

Peter Spellmeyer, "Sport Hunting Can Indeed Save Endangered Species," *Virginian-Pilot*, October 24, 2003.

Rob Stein, "Research Shows Dogs Have Inborn Talent to 'Read' Humans," *Virginian-Pilot*, August 22, 2003.

Interview

Lisa Lange, vice president of communications of People for the Ethical Treatment of Animals (PETA), Norfolk, VA, December 2, 2003.

Internet Sources

American Humane Association, "Protecting Animals in Film and Television," www.ahafilm.org/history.html.

American Meat Institute, "The Ethical and Economic Reasons to Treat Animals Humanely," www.meatami.com/content/presscenter/factsheets_Infokits/ EthicalandEconomic ReasonstoTreatAnimalsHumanely.pdf.

America's Charities, "Humane Society of the United States," www.charities.org/member/hsus.html.

Animal Protection Institute, "Exposing the Myths: The Truth About Trapping," November 19, 2001. www.api4animals.org/doc.asp?ID=1123.

Ellin Beltz, "1987 HerPET-POURRI," May 1987. www.ebeltz.net/column/1987colu.html.

Mary Carmichael, "Animal Emotions," MSNBC, July 21, 2003. www.msnbc.com.

Center for Laboratory Animal Welfare, "Overview of Animals in Laboratories," www.labanimalwelfare.org.

Gary Diamond, "Mid-Atlantic 2003 Outlook," *Mid-Atlantic Game & Fish*, October 5, 2003. www.midatlanticgameand fish.com/at_aa100503a.

Elephant Sanctuary in Tennessee, "Feds Fine Deland-Based Circus for Beating Elephant," December 24, 2003. www.elephants.com/globalnews_circus_03.htm#feds.

Faye Flam, "Study: Animals Used to Roaming Fare Badly at Zoos," *Philadelphia Inquirer*, October 2, 2003. www.philly.com/mld/inquirer/news/front/6910373.htm.

Foundation for Animal Use in Education, "Animals in Entertainments," www.animaluse.org/html/animals_entertain.html.

Tim Franks, "EU Bans Animal Testing for Cosmetics," BBC, January 15, 2003. http://news.bbc.co.uk/2/hi/europe/2661797.stm.

Fur Commission USA, "Fur Retail Sales Remain Strong in Unstable Economy," May 20, 2002. www.furcommission.com/news/newsF04w.htm.

Greyhound Racing Association of America, "Training at the Tracks," www.gra-america.org/training.html.

Humane Society of the United States, "Greyhound Racing Facts," www.hsus.org/ace/11798.

———, "Learn the Facts About Hunting," www.hsus.org/ace/12043?pg=3.

———, "An Overview of Animal Testing Issues," http://files.hsus.org/web-files/PDF/ARIS_An_ Overview_Of_Animal_Testing_Issues.pdf.

———, "Whistleblower Draws Scrutiny to Columbia University," October 2003. www.hsus.org/ace/20019.

Institute for Animal Rights Law, "Some Thoughts on the Rights of Animals," www.instituteforanimalrightslaw.org/articles_thoughts_on_animal_rights.htm.

Johns Hopkins Center for Alternatives to Animal Testing, "CAAT 20th Anniversary Symposium," September 2001. http://caat.jhsph.edu/programs/workshops/20th/schwetz.htm.

Jeff Johnson, "'Animal Rights' Group Promotes Criminal 'Achievements,'" CNS News, January 22, 2002. www.cnsnews.com.

Nicole Kraft, "Lasix," U.S. Trotting Association, www.ustrotting. com/hoofbeats/lasix-ma.htm.

Marsha Laux, "Pastured Poultry Industry Profile," Agricultural Marketing Research Center, October 2003. www.agmrc.org.

Delia Montgomery, "Fur Ethics," Fur Commission USA, November 2001. www.furcommission.com/resource/perspect999as.htm.

National Academy of Sciences, "Guide for the Care and Use of Laboratory Animals," 1996. www.nap.edu/readingroom/books/labrats.

National Anti-Vivisection Society, "Animals in Education," www.navs.org/education/dissection_hotline.cfm?SectionID=Education.

National Association of Biology Teachers, "The Use of Animals in Biology Education," www.nabt.org/sub/position_statements/animals.asp.

National Humane Education Society, "Dog and Horse Racing," www.nhes.org/articles.asp?article_id=222&section_id=60.

National Pork Producers Council, "Voluntary Reforms in the Livestock Industry Have Changed the Way Animals Are Slaughtered," April 28, 2003. www.nppc.org/news/stories/2003/030429Welfare.html.

National Rifle Association, "Hunter Services: Facts & Frequently Asked Questions," www.nrahq.org/hunting/hunter dollars.asp.

Amanda Onion, "Hunt and Protect?" ABC News, May 7, 2002. http://abcnews.go.com/sections/scitech/DailyNews/sheephunting020507.html.

Rose Palazzalo, "Animal Testing for Cosmetics Decreasing," ABC News, www.abcnews.com.

PBS, "A Whale of a Business," 1998. www.pbs.org/wgbh/pages/frontline/shows/whales.

Ringling Bros. and Barnum & Bailey, "Amazing Animals," www.ringling.com/animals.

John Scheiman, "Horses, Drugs Are Racing's Daily Double; No Uniform Policy in Industry," *Washington Post*, April 27, 2003. www.washingtonpost.com.

William S. Stokes, "The Role of ICCVAM in Evaluating New and Alternative Test Methods," *Lab Animal*, 2002. www.labanimal.com.

Carolyn Stull, Richard Warner, and Lowell Wilson, "Special Fed Veal," http://ars.sdstate.edu/animaliss/veal.html.

Susan Thomas, "Industries Test Cosmetics on Animals," *Florida Today*, June 30, 2002. www.floridatoday.com/news/verge/stories/2002/june/063002second.htm.

C.B. Tucker and D.M. Weary, "Tail Docking in Dairy Cattle," *Animal Welfare Information Center Bulletin*, Winter 2001–Spring 2002. www.nal.usda.gov/awic/newsletters/ v11n3/11n3 tuck.htm.

United Egg Producers, "Animal Husbandry Guidelines Overview of Best Management Practices for United States Egg Laying Flocks," 2003. www.unitedegg.org/html/welfare/animal husbandry.pdf.

Judy Wieder, "Melissa Etheridge: The Advocate's Person of the Year," *Advocate*, January 23, 1998. www.advocate.com/html/specials/melissa/698_99_melissa.asp.

Web Sites

American Humane Association (AHA) Film and Television Unit (www.ahafilm.org). AHA is dedicated to ensuring animals used in television and films are not mistreated. AHA has set guidelines that filmmakers must follow to receive AHA accreditation and discusses these guidelines on its Web site.

Animal and Plant Health Inspection Service (APHIS) (www.aphis.usda.gov). APHIS is the division of the USDA that oversees the inspectors required by the Animal Welfare Act and addresses animal care issues.

Animal Welfare Information Center (www.awic.org). This Web site provides an online library of USDA information and publications regarding improved animal care and use in research, teaching, and testing.

Hollywood Animals' Animal Actor Agency (www.animal actorsgency.com). This organization supplies exotic and domestic animals to film, television, and industries. Its sources are private owners and wild animals in captivity. Its Web site discusses how the agency works and lists the animals it has access to.

Performing Animal Welfare Society (PAWS) (www.paws web.org). PAWS provides homes for abandoned or abused performing animals and victims of the exotic animal trade.

Index

Picture Credits

Cover photo: © Charles E. Rotkin/CORBIS
AP/Wide World Photos, 11, 35, 40, 61, 72, 78
© Bettmann/CORBIS, 18, 23, 47, 64, 84
© Christie's Images/CORBIS, 14
Corel Corporation, 36 (background)
Farm Sanctuary, 28, 31
© Ed Kashi/CORBIS, 43
© Dan Lamont/CORBIS, 21
© Robert Maass/CORBIS, 52 (background)
© Wally McNamee/CORBIS, 57
Photos.com, 27, 48, 67, 73, 77, 81
© Reuters/CORBIS, 17
© Charles E. Rotkin/CORBIS, 58
© Bob Rowan; Progressive Image/CORBIS, 9
© Galen Rowell/CORBIS, 85
© RPG/Roman Poderny/CORBIS SYGMA, 53
© Steve Starr/CORBIS, 70
Steve Zmina, 36, 39, 44, 52

About the Author

Leanne K. Currie-McGhee's articles and stories have appeared in *Pockets*, *Guideposts for Kids*, and *Highlights for Children*. She is also the author of *Gun Control* published by Lucent Books. Ms. Currie-McGhee resides in Norfolk, Virginia, with her husband, Keith, and daughter, Grace.